CRIMINAL JUSTICE AND CRIMINOLOGY

A Career Guide to Local, State, Federal, and Academic Positions

James F. Anderson
Nancie J. Mangels
Laronistine Dyson

University Press of America,® Inc.
Dallas · Lanham · Boulder · New York · Oxford

Copyright © 2003 by
University Press of America,® Inc.
4501 Forbes Boulevard
Suite 200
Lanham, Maryland 20706
UPA Acquisitions Department (301) 459-3366

PO Box 317
Oxford
OX2 9RU, UK

ISBN 0-7618-2761-7 (paperback : alk. ppr.)

⊖™ The paper used in this publication meets the minimum
requirements of American National Standard for Information
Sciences—Permanence of Paper for Printed Library Materials,
ANSI Z39.48—1984

TABLE OF CONTENTS

PREFACE

What can one do with a degree in criminal justice or criminology? The average student or potential major would probably think of policing, or possibly becoming a correctional officer in a prison. Because of this, some students might shy away from criminal justice or criminology as a major or even refrain from taking a criminal justice course. Yet, there are a multitude of job positions for which a criminal justice or criminology degree prepares students, from criminal justice related positions to research and teaching. Criminal Justice & Criminology: A Career Guide to Local, State, Federal, and Academic Positions provides undergraduate and graduate students with more than one hundred pages of specific job announcements, plus a wealth of information on gaining a teaching or research position at a college, university or research agency. In addition, the text includes candid interviews with actual criminal justice practitioners. Much of the information provided could only be gained previously from devoted teaching mentors who possess — invaluable information that all students need, yet many do not receive. As such, this text will benefit any criminal justice student whether undergraduate or graduate. At the same time, others with an interest in justice-related employment could benefit by reading this book.

Part One of this text provides an overview of the criminal justice system, including the police, courts, corrections, and the juvenile justice system. It also provides an overview of major research institutions. A section on academic teaching positions provides a detailed explanation of the ranking system in colleges and universities; invaluable strategies on searching for employment; choosing a suitable college or university; interviewing for a teaching position; negotiating salary and benefits; and lateral moves within academia. This section also lists more than 150 criminal justice/criminology programs by school, the degrees offered, and whether the programs are focused on teaching or research so that graduate students can apply for teaching positions at the school that is right for them.

Part Two lists specific job positions in criminal justice with information related to duties, qualifications, educational requirements; skills needed for each position; what to expect in the hiring process; and salary range. Part Three provides the same information for teaching positions in two year and four year colleges and provides an extensive list of contact information for criminal justice departments and programs.

Part Four includes a discussion of major U.S. research institutes and lists research positions at these institutes that would be appropriate for criminal justice majors. Part Five consists of interviews with selected practitioners in the field, plus an interview with a professor at a four year college. Respondents were interviewed using an open-ended format in order to increase the validity of the information provided. The survey for the interviews contained twenty-three items, such as (1) how many hours per week they typically work; (2) the effects of their career on family time; (3) the number of years needed before retirement; (4) promotion and location; and (5) risks on the job. In addition, they were asked (1) what they liked best and least about the job; (2) their daily routine; (3) pay scale for their position; (4) educational background; (5) what type of person they feel is best suited for this career; (6) personal satisfaction, and other pertinent questions.

This section gives students an idea of what it is actually like to do each job on a day-to-day basis. Of the many positions found in the area of criminal justice, a representative group was chosen for the interviews, consisting of a full professor, retired FBI agent, male and female police officers, probation officer, correctional officer, crime scene investigator, parole officer, state trooper, and a juvenile probation officer. Most students would never have the chance to interview criminal justice practitioners in this manner, so this section gives them an opportunity to read what may be surprising answers to questions that will help them decide if they would be suited for a particular criminal justice or criminology career.

For many students, television is their primary source of information about crime and the criminal justice system. While the entertainment media has done much to stimulate interest in criminal justice employment (e.g. crime scene investigator, detective, criminal profiler, forensic investigator, and attorney), they often distort the reality of what the jobs actually entail. The goal of this text is to present a wide spectrum of careers related to criminology and criminal justice in order to provide students with an abundance of career options and realistic information about the duties associated with the positions. After reading this text, students will be aware of the many career opportunities that are available if they select criminal justice or criminology as their area of study. At the same time, they will have an understanding of the duties and responsibilities that are part of the job.

James F. Anderson
Nancie J. Mangels
University of Missouri - Kansas City
Missouri
2003

Laronistine Dyson
Residential Alternatives Inc.
Kentucky
2003

INTRODUCTION

Crime and criminal behavior are fascinating aspects of the human experience. The issue of crime has never been as popular in the nation's history as it is now. In fact, the attention given to crime by local and national news mediums consumes a disproportionate amount of air time. Concurrently, the entertainment medium has capitalized on crime and justice with such programming as *Court TV; America's Most Wanted; The Practice; COPS; Law and Order: Crime Scene Investigation; FBI Files; Homicide;* and *Profiler* to name only a few. For many people, crime is a social reality that is both horrendous and yet intriguing. For example, we feel sympathetic toward crime victims, yet we are fascinated by the kinds of people who commit crime, especially those that are gruesome and shocking to our conscience. As concerned citizens, we wonder where these people come from and what life experiences they had that eventually manifested in fatal episodes of crime and violence. Perhaps the fascination that many of us have is fueled by the new technologies used to bring criminal offenders to justice. In recent times, DNA evidence has gone from being esoteric to being universally recognized and accepted. Again, the mass media presents a variety of docudramas devoted to crime scene investigations and criminal profiles. In these programs, crime news is prepackaged to provide *infotainment*. Such programming, while informative, may actually feed our fascination and desire to know more about crime and the people who engage in such behavior. Crime is an inescapable reality with which society must deal. Because of this, many people have devoted their lives to crime prevention. In doing so, they hope to alleviate much of the pain and suffering associated with the human condition.

Arguably, the main attractions that draw students to criminal justice and criminology are twofold: (1) Students can quickly acquire employment after graduation, and (2) they can see the immediate impact of their labor. First, quick employment is extremely important to many students who ponder the prospect of accumulating more debt. However, for other students, this is far from reality since they (based on the area of study) must pursue a graduate education after four years of undergraduate studies to enter the career of their choice. This can be exceedingly burdensome and expensive to students who have already received loans or those who desire to join the ranks of the labor force, start their careers and families, or pursue their dreams. Second, by working in an area of justice, employees see first hand the impact of their involvement and how it can help to prevent and alleviate pain and suffering that victims experience.

Those students who seemingly select criminal justice or criminology as a major may be unaware that it is the discipline that selects the student. For example, the overwhelming majority of students who major in one of the aforementioned social sciences often do so because of personal reasons and their concerns about justice and equality before the law. After enrolling in an introductory course, they quickly discover that they have concerns about fundamental fairness guaranteed by the U.S. Constitution to everyone who enters the American criminal justice system or they are disturbed by the lack of attention afforded to the victims of crime. Their curiosity could also be piqued because they either know someone who was processed in the system or they have friends or loved ones who have been the victim of a crime. Another popular view is that they also may have been a crime victim. Because of these reasons, some students eventually attend graduate school to increase their knowledge base of criminal justice or criminology. This is indicated by the rise in student enrollment over the years (Schmalleger, 2001).

Students who major in criminal justice embark on the study of the agencies of social control at the local, state, and federal levels. These agencies include police, courts, corrections, and the juvenile justice system. Students learn that these agencies are charged with dispensing justice to those with which they have interactions. Stated another way, students of justice learn how the agencies of social control operate in a democratic society. They quickly learn that the tasks that confront the criminal justice system are twofold: (1) to protect the rights of individual offenders, and (2) to advocate the public order mandate or promote community safety. Those who graduate with advanced degrees in criminal justice are referred to as criminal justicians or criminal justice experts. On the other hand, students majoring in criminology embark on the study of an interdisciplinary science that relies upon biology, psychology, political science, economics, sociology, and anthropology to explain crime and deviant behavior. Students of criminology are concerned with using the scientific approach to study the causes of crime. They examine the nature and extent of the crime problem in America to determine if the crime rate is increasing or declining. They also are concerned with how society reacts and responds to crime and criminal behavior. They seek to identify, describe, predict, explain, and ultimately control criminal behavior. Unlike undergraduates, those who graduate with advanced degrees in criminology are referred to as criminologists. They could specialize in one or more of the following areas: criminal statistics; sociology of law; theory construction; criminal behavior systems; penology; or victimology.

Criminal justice and criminology as academic disciplines are not mutually exclusive per se, but rather they depend on each other. Students majoring in either discipline will be required to take courses in the other area of study. Moreover, those criminal justicians who have custody of offenders often treat them based on policy recommendations given by criminologists who endeavor to isolate crime-producing factors. For example, penal experts who oversee the operations of boot camps may integrate strategies suggested by researchers who study the behavior of offenders. On the other hand, criminologists often monitor what occurs to inmates while they are in penal custody to determine if the practices used by criminal justice experts help to either promote recidivism or reduce the prospect of reoffending.

This book provides criminal justice and criminology majors with a list of areas they can pursue as possible careers. The book is divided into five parts. Part One provides an introduction to both the criminal justice and juvenile justice systems. It also offers suggestions to those either pursuing a doctorate degree in criminal justice or criminology or those who may hold the terminal degree and are interested in an academic or research position. Part Two lists and provides a description of jobs for which students may qualify after receiving a bachelor's or master's degree. This section lists local, state, and federal jobs. Part Three lists and provides a description of research jobs for which students may qualify after receiving a bachelor's, masters, or doctorate degree. These positions include state, federal, and academic assignments. Part Four lists and provides a description of academic teaching positions which require a master's and/or doctorate degree for both community colleges and four year colleges and universities. Part Five presents interviews taken from criminal justice practitioners who have worked in their respective areas for several years.

PART ONE
The Criminal Justice System

THE CRIMINAL JUSTICE SYSTEM

The criminal justice system, in general, seeks to apprehend, prosecute, adjudicate, sentence, and punish or rehabilitate criminal offenders in an equitable manner. The justice system includes agencies that can be divided into three areas: police, courts, and corrections. First, police are charged with serving and protecting the community. They investigate crimes and make arrests based on a finding of probable cause. *Probable cause* is the level of proof that leads an officer to believe that a person engaged in a crime. Any physical or testimonial evidence collected by police at a crime scene will be used against the suspect in a court of law. Second, courts try cases when there is a showing that a prima facie case can be made by the prosecutor. A *prima facie* case is one that proceeds with sufficient evidence that a crime has been committed by the defendant. Third, corrections are places to where the criminally accused are sentenced after a judge or jury has determined guilt and pronounced sentence. The agencies of the system are responsible for delivering justice to the criminal suspect on one level or another. The system is characterized by federalism, which allows justice to be dispensed on the state and federal levels. Each component of the system (i.e., police, court, and corrections) can be found on the federal, state, and local levels. The justice system seeks to dispense justice and fundamental fairness as required by both state and national constitutions. The system is actually challenged by protecting the community interests and safeguarding the constitutional and civil rights of criminal offenders.

POLICE

Of the components in the criminal justice system, the police are the most visible. This is probably because they are the first agency to respond to calls or complaints about crime, not to mention that there are an estimated 17,500 police agencies in the U.S. employing over 800,000 persons. They are the first line of defense when it comes to investigating and solving crime. They apprehend and arrest suspects and bring them into the justice system. Consequently, police are referred to as the "gate-keepers" of the criminal justice system. Gaines, Kuane, and Miller (2000) argue that there are 12,502 municipal police departments; 3,086 sheriff's departments; 1,721 special police agencies limited to policing parks; schools; and airports; 49 state police departments; and 50 federal law enforcement agencies.

Inciardi (1999) contends that the general functions of police are to (1) protect constitutional guarantees of free speech and assembly; (2) facilitate movement of people and vehicles; (3) resolve conflict; (4) identify problems; (5) create and maintain feelings of security in the community; and (6) assist those who cannot care for themselves. More specifically, police functions are threefold: (1) maintain public order, (2) enforce the criminal laws, and (3) provide service. First, an important task of police is to maintain domestic order. This function is primarily concerned with preventing disturbances and threats to public tranquility. Police are allowed to use discretion to accomplish this result and other objectives (Smith, 1998). Second, the chief task of police is to enforce the criminal law. When law violations occur, police must swiftly react by investigating and ascertaining facts and make arrests when possible to bring the guilty to justice. This function of policing is sometimes delayed because victims and or witnesses may fail to report crimes that have been committed against them or in their presence. Third, police spend a tremendous amount of time providing services. Such a function may include providing first aid to people who are in immediate need of care. They also rescue animals, and extend social services to citizens, such as intervening in domestic violence and child abuse when needed. They assist communities in their efforts to fight crime by checking the doors of buildings, and assisting with runaways and drunks. This is not meant to be an exhaustive representation of the services police provide.

Federal Law Enforcement Agencies

Federal agencies have been authorized by Congress to enforce specific laws. The U.S. Department of Justice is the primary federal law enforcement agency in the country. While more glamorous than policing on the state and local levels, they are considerably smaller. Experts argue that their appeal and mystique is due in large part to Hollywood's depiction of the operations of this agency. Law enforcement agencies found on the federal level include the Federal Bureau of Investigation (FBI); Drug Enforcement Administration (DEA); Bureau of Alcohol, Tobacco, and Firearms (ATF). Some others are the Secret Service Division of the Treasury Department (responsible for counterfeiting, forgery, protector of the President), the Internal Revenue Service (IRS); U.S. Marshals; Bureau of Postal Inspection; Border Patrol; the Bureau of Citizenship and Immigration Services (BCIS) formerly the Division of Immigration and Naturalization Services (INS); National Parks Services;

and the International Police (INTERPOL).

State Law Enforcement Agencies

With the exception of Hawaii, all other states in the U.S. have a state police. State agencies have two types of police: state police and highway patrol. These police officers have a different level of authority and jurisdiction. Perhaps the best known of all state police are the Texas Rangers. The state police primarily assists local police agencies that lack adequate resources to handle certain law enforcement tasks. State police have statewide jurisdiction and are legally authorized to perform a variety of law enforcement tasks. On the other hand, highway police have limited authority. They are either limited by jurisdiction or by types of offenses they have the authority to control (Gaines et al., 2000). They investigate criminal activities that cross jurisdictional boundaries, such as when robbers commit crime in one county and flee to another county in the same state. They provide law enforcement in rural and other areas that do not have local or county police help.

County Law Enforcement Agencies

County policing is the primary jurisdiction of the sheriff's department. Sheriff's departments vary in size and resources. It is estimated that there are 3,086 sheriff's departments in the U.S. Most sheriff's departments are assigned their duties by state law. It is estimated that 90 percent of all sheriff's departments have the primary responsibility of investigating violent crimes in their jurisdictions. The duties performed by the sheriff's department include: protecting the public; serving as county jail administrator; and carrying out civil and criminal processes within county lines. They perform multiple functions, such as serve eviction notices and court summons; keep order in county courthouses; collect taxes; and enforce orders of the court such as overseeing the sequestration of a jury during a trial (Cole, 1995). The sheriff's department is very involved in operating local jails.

Municipal Law Enforcement Agencies

Municipal policing represents the overwhelming majority of police work in small and medium sized police departments. Municipal police have the broadest authority to catch criminal suspects, maintain order, and provide community service. Like sheriff's departments, local police officers perform many of the same functions. Municipal officers receive and dispatch calls for service; investigate crime; conduct routine patrol;

provide court security; operate jails; engage in search and rescue operations; take fingerprints; enforce traffic laws; investigate accidents; and direct traffic and patrol. Local police spend a tremendous amount of time on traffic control.

COURTS

Courts are places where legal disputes are settled. Because of federalism, the court system in the U.S. extends to both the state and federal levels. Courts can be defined as public judiciaries with a judge or judges with the authority to hand down rulings and decisions on legal conflict and issues through the application of law (Anderson and Dyson, 2001). There are a number of actors in the court process: judge, prosecutor, defense attorney, bailiff, and court reporter. They compose what is referred to as a courtroom workgroup. Judges are officers of the court who ensure that proper legal procedures are followed before, doing, and after a trial. Judges are also responsible for managing case dockets. Prosecutors are officers of the court who endeavor to successfully represent the state by convicting suspects who have violated the laws of a given jurisdiction. They often work directly with police. Defense attorneys are officers of the court who advocate and properly defend clients in matters of the law. Bailiffs are employees of the court who are responsible for providing protection to the judge and maintaining order during the court process. The court clerk is a court employee who transcribes all verbal statements made during court proceedings (Gaines et al, 2000). Taken together, the efforts of the court workgroup allow for the quick disposition of case dockets.

Federal Courts

Unlike other legal systems, U.S. courts are decentralized. The federal court system is composed of a three-tier system: the Supreme Court, federal circuit courts, and district courts. The Supreme Court is the highest court in the nation. This Court decides which cases to hear from both the federal and state courts. The decisions of the Court could be the basis of public policy that will ultimately impact the entire nation. There is only one Supreme Court with nine justices presiding. The Court is composed of one Chief Justice and eight associate justices who are appointed by the President with the approval and consent of the U.S. Senate. They are tenured for life. There are thirteen U.S. Courts of Appeals, often referred to as circuit courts. They have jurisdiction over all cases appealed from the 94 federal district courts. All states in the U.S. have jurisdiction in one of the thirteen circuit courts of appeal. The President, with the approval and consent of the Senate, appoints all circuit court judges. They, too, are tenured for life. Each state has at least one circuit court, while some states (e.g. Texas, California, New York), may have as many as three courts depending on the size of the state. District courts are trial courts on the federal level. They are places where cases are initially filed and tried. The President, with the approval and consent of the Senate, appoints district court judges. In the federal court system, every judge is nominated by the President and approved and confirmed by the U.S. Senate (Schmalleger, 2001).

State Courts
    The state court system is unique in that each state has a separate system. However, there are three tiers found in the state system. They include a state supreme court or appellate court, trial court of general jurisdiction, and a trial court of limited jurisdiction. First, state supreme courts or appellate courts (varies within states), are referred to as the court of the last resort. It has discretion to decide what cases it will hear. Where the issue is concerned with a matter of state law or state constitution, the state supreme court has the final say. Unless the state law or constitution runs counter to the national Constitution, the state supreme court has sovereign jurisdiction (Anderson and Dyson, 2001). Second, trial courts of general jurisdiction are concerned with trial cases regarding criminal and civil matters. These courts are referred to as felony courts. Most cases tried in these courts focus on personal and property crimes. Where a civil matter is concerned, the dollar amount determines which court will have jurisdiction over the matter. Third, courts of limited jurisdiction are limited to hearing misdemeanors: formal charges against accused persons, holding preliminary hearings, and some trials for minor offenses. On the state level, judges are selected from several processes that range from partisan elections to executive appointment and nonpartisan elections to the Missouri Plan. State judges are not tenured for life (Gaines et al., 2000).

CORRECTIONS

The third component in the criminal justice system is corrections.

After the trial process is completed, a judge (if there is a bench trial) or a jury determines whether the offender is guilty of committing a crime. If guilt is determined, sentence is pronounced and the offender is remanded to the state department of corrections. In some cases, depending on the seriousness of the crime and the offender's criminal past, probation may be imposed. If probation is imposed, the offender is placed under the authority of the department of probation. While serving probation, the offender must not recidivate and must adhere to the conditions of probation. The offender remains in the free community until he or she engages in a new crime or violates a condition of probation. Essentially, corrections involve the type of punishment offenders serve while in state or federal custody. Similar to police and courts, corrections is also structured. For example, there is a federal corrections system, plus state corrections systems, community corrections, private prisons, and local jails. One important fact of corrections is that facilities and inmates are classified in a security-level system that ranges from level 1 (the least secure, camp-type setting, such as the Federal Prison Camp) to level 6 (the most secure U.S. Penitentiary).

Federal prison populations contain inmates who have been convicted of white-collar crimes (although the number of drug offenders is increasing in federal prisons). Federal prisons typically have jurisdiction over nonviolent offenders. However, each of the 50 states and the District of Columbia has a centralized department of corrections. State prisons contain violent offenders. Another popular form of punishment is community corrections. It includes probation, intermediate sanctions, and parole (due to prison overcrowding, offenders fulfill their sentences in the community). Participants of community correction programs are typically viewed as nonviolent and nonthreatening. There are more inmates sentenced to community corrections than the other forms of traditional incarceration combined. In fact, experts suggest that an estimated 4 million offenders are under some form of community supervision program. After time served, the majority of inmates will be eligible for parole unless specified by their sentence. If parole is granted, the offenders must adhere to the conditions of parole and must not reoffend. Failure to adhere to conditions of release and engaging in new crimes will mean that the offender's status of parole will be revoked, and he or she will be returned to prison. Both probation and parole are aimed at reintegrating the offender back into conventional society.

Prison Classification

State prison systems are adult institutions that range in scope. They include facilities and programs such as prisons; reformatories; industrial institutions; prison farms; conservation campuses; forestry campuses; and halfway houses. Maximum security prisons hold 26 percent of state inmates. They are typically built like fortresses, surrounded by stone walls with guard towers and are designed to prevent escapes. They house the most violent offenders such as murderers, rapists, child molesters, and drug offenders. Medium security prisons hold 49 percent of state inmates. They, too, are typically built like maximum-security prisons. However, there is great emphasis placed on treatment and rehabilitation. Offenders sentenced to these institutions are given some privileges and contact with the outside world through routine visitation and other freedoms. Minimum security prisons hold 25 percent of state inmates. Offenders sentenced to these prisons are usually the least violent offenders. In fact, some of the offenders have committed white-collar crimes. These prisons lack stone walls and a guard watch tower. Instead, offenders live dormitory style or in small private rooms without barred walls, and are allowed many freedoms.

Private Prisons

Private prisons are correctional facilities that are owned and operated by private businesses. The first adult prison opened in Kentucky in 1985. By 1994, there were an estimated 88 private prisons for adults with a capacity to hold 49,000 in the 18 states that had them. It is believed that the private prison industry is dominated by two companies: Corrections Corporation of America and Wackenhut. Private prisons, like other prisons, have their share of criticisms. For example, some questions of major concern are: Who is legally responsible if inmates escape and cause harm to citizens? What type of offenders are admitted to these facilities? Are they an appropriate agency to have a social control function? Do they function with the interest of the public in mind? Are their employees and county safe from inmate uprising? Do they deliver quality services, especially supervision? Again, major concerns linger over whether businesses can effectively and inexpensively run safe private prisons, and whether private businesses (rather than the state) should be involved in the deprivation of liberty.

Local Jails

Jails function primarily to hold persons awaiting trial and offenders who have been sentenced. It is estimated that there are 3,300 locally administered jails in the U.S. They are places designed as detention centers for suspects awaiting trial, penal institutions for offenders found guilty of misdemeanors who have received a sentence of less than a year and lock-up for social misfits who are taken off the streets (i.e., drunks, homeless, prostitutes, mental patients, etc.). As stated earlier, the sheriff's departments and local law enforcement agencies typically run jails. To many experts, jails serve multiple correctional functions since half of jail inmates are sentenced offenders under correctional authority. Despite their primary function, prison overcrowding has required jails to hold felony offenders who have been sentenced to a state prison, but cannot be turned over to the state's department of corrections due to a lack of bed space. Moreover, jails are being used to house persons awaiting transportation to prison and persons convicted of parole or probation violation.

THE JUVENILE JUSTICE SYSTEM

Juveniles are an important aspect of the criminal justice system since they engage in a disproportionate number of crime and figure prominently in arrest, crime, and victimization statistics as indicated by the Uniform Crime Reports (UCR), Self-Report Surveys (SRS), and the National Crime Victimization Survey (NCVS). However, juvenile justice, and the court systems created to process children who break the law, can be very confusing and difficult fields to understand, because when the District of Columbia is considered, there are fifty-one separate juvenile justice systems in the United States. Each state has a different juvenile justice system. The National Center for Juvenile Justice (NCJJ), report that most states deliver services on two levels: local and state. For example, some juvenile justice services are provided at the local juvenile court level while other services are provided at the state level (2002). Essentially, juvenile justice uses a dual system that has two separate and distinct juvenile justice programs within the state. In most cases, duties such as screening and probation services are provided at the local court level while secure confinement and aftercare services of juveniles are provided at the state level (Griffin, 2000). Despite this, states vary in terms of which agency will administer services and oversee the various juvenile agencies (NCJJ, 2002).

The Juvenile Courts

When juveniles engage in crime or status offenses, the juvenile justice process is activated. Most juveniles come to the attention of the local juvenile court. According to the NCJJ, the most common approach to processing juveniles is to give the local juvenile courts administrative powers over juvenile probation services (NCJJ, 2002). While juvenile probation departments do not provide the same function, generally speaking, the duties of the juvenile probation department include screening cases that are referred to juvenile court (intake), pre-disposition investigations and community supervision of juveniles placed on probation (Torbet, 1996). However, some probation departments do not provide intake duties, nor share the responsibility for intake with prosecutors. Some probation departments have the responsibility of running a detention center or local residential center (Torbet, 1996). At the local level, juveniles experience: intake, transfer, detention, adjudication and disposition hearings, and diversion. At the state level, juveniles experience commitment and aftercare (Whitehead and Lab, 1990; Senna and Siegel, 2000; Gaines et al., 2001).

Intake

Juveniles may experience intake after they have committed crimes or status offenses and the police officer believes that formal actions should be taken by the juvenile justice system. After apprehension, the police officer files a complaint with a special division of the juvenile probation department for preliminary screening and evaluation (Cole and Smith, 1998). The intake process is primarily concerned with whether the alleged facts are sufficient to cause the juvenile court to take jurisdiction over the matter, or decide whether some other course of action would be in the best interests of the juvenile. According to Bartollas and Miller (2001), the intake process functions to screen cases for the juvenile court by determining if a child needs to come to the attention of the juvenile court, and to dispose of cases that do not. In most cases, a probation officer, a prosecutor, or both are major actors in the intake process. During intake, informal discussions usually take place between the probation officer and prosecutor. They often discuss the child's situation, behavioral problems, and treatment recommendations (Cole and Smith, 1998). If a petition is filed against the juvenile by a probation officer, it requires the approval of an attorney, the juvenile prosecutor. Intake workers have many options that they can choose from that would not send a child to court. First, the case could be dismissed, with an informal adjustment ordered (which is the process of getting the youth into diversion or restitution or other programs without a formal adjudication). Second, informal probation could be ordered which would require the child to be placed under the supervision of court without a finding of delinquency. Third, a consent decree could be issued. This document places the child under court jurisdiction to fulfill certain requirements without a formal adjudication. Finally, the intake worker could request that a petition be filed with the juvenile court and that the child come to court to answer allegations of delinquent conduct (Bartollas and Miller, 2001).

Transfer

Juveniles may be transferred to adult court through a process of judicial waiver (Cole and Smith, 1998). Most states allow older offenders to be waived to the adult system. Some factors that typically lead juveniles to be transferred to the adult system are crime seriousness and routine encounters with the juvenile courts, or when a judge believes that another juvenile court effort is not going to solve the juvenile's problem (Whitehead and Lab, 1990). A juvenile waiver is typically made at a hearing that is similar to a preliminary hearing in the adult system (Cole and Smith, 1998). At the hearing, the prosecutor must show probable cause and that the juvenile committed the offense. Prosecutors do not have to prove guilt beyond a reasonable doubt to have a juvenile transferred into the adult system. Proof of guilt is reserved for the adult trial if the waiver is granted. After a finding of probable cause, the juvenile judge makes the decision to transfer the minor to the adult court. Again, this is typically based on crime seriousness, a judge's belief that the juvenile is not amenable to juvenile court intervention, or the juvenile is a continued threat to the general public (Whitehead and Lab, 1990). If the juvenile is transferred to the criminal justice system, he or she becomes subject to adult penalties such as a lengthy sentence of imprisonment at a traditional institution with other adults (Whitehead and Lab, 1990). Such actions could have serious consequences on the juvenile since it accompanies an adult criminal record which is public and will follow the juvenile for life. At the same time, the young offender may be at the mercy of predatory adult offenders in prison. In the past, juvenile court records were confidential, sealed, and sometimes expunged. Today, however, some have moved towards opening juvenile records (Torbet and Szymanski, 1998).

Detention

During the juvenile justice process, some offenders are held in secure confinement. As a general rule, juveniles should not be held in adult jails. Juvenile detention centers are used for juveniles who must be held securely (Reddington and Anderson, 1996). The primary purpose of a detention facility is to hold children in a secure setting while they await an adjudication hearing or placement as part of their disposition (Griffin, 2000). Harms (2002) reports that about nineteen percent of juveniles referred to juvenile courts in 1998 spent time in a detention center. A growing trend is to use detention itself as a disposition for a juvenile offender, much like we use jail as a disposition in the adult system (Griffin, 2000).

Adjudication and Disposition

For juveniles who are not waived to the adult system, a petition alleging delinquent conduct is filed, and the juvenile is scheduled for adjudication and a disposition hearing. In the adjudication hearings, a judge uses the evidence presented by the prosecution to assess the merits of the case. Essentially, a judge must establish whether the evidence presented against a juvenile is strong enough to adjudicate the child as delinquent. The adjudication process is comparable to the adult trial (See Whitehead and Lab, 1990) and generally the actors in the proceedings are a judge, a prosecutor, and a defense lawyer. After the adjudication hearing, a disposition hearing occurs. A disposition hearing in juvenile court focuses on the sentencing aspect of the proceeding. In this process, a judge considers reports provided by the probation officer. Some scholars (Thornberry, 1973; Thomas and Cage, 1977; Staples, 1987) argue that the sentencing decision is based on a number of factors such as crime seriousness, prior record, and extralegal variable such as age, race, gender, and social class. Other scholars contend that dispositions are complex and typically vary from one jurisdiction to another (e.g., Belknap, 1984; Dannefer and Schutt, 1982). The result is a disposition plan created to help the young offender to overcome behavior problems, and to protect the community. In most jurisdictions, disposition includes the payment of a fine, probation, drug and alcohol treatment, foster care, victim restitution, community service or a combination of these sanctions. It could also include confinement in a juvenile detention center, or in a residential facility (Light, 1999).

Diversion Programs

Diversion programs have increased dramatically in recent years (Gaines et al., 2001). They are given to juveniles who would not benefit from traditional processing by the juvenile justice system. They may also be given to young offenders who do not require the overall services of juvenile court, probation, and corrections (see Coffey, 1972). For example, they could be given to those who live in troubled environments. A diversion is an alternative course of action used to remove a low risk offender from the juvenile justice system. There are several categories of diversion programs: probation, treatment and aid, and restitution. Under probation, the juvenile is returned to the community under the supervision of a juvenile probation officer. If the juvenile breaks a condition of probation or commits additional crimes, he or she will be returned to the formal juvenile system. Treatment and aid programs are designed for juvenile offenders with medical and behavioral problems. Some programs offer remedial education, drug and alcohol treatment, and other forms of counseling to alleviate these problems (Cole and Smith, 1998). In restitution programs, offenders "repay" their victim directly or through providing community services.

Commitment

In some cases, juveniles cannot be kept in the local juvenile justice system because their crimes are too serious, or their behavior is not amenable to change through the resources of the local courts. These juveniles are committed to the youth correctional system. These systems are usually overseen by the state. In seventeen states, the state system serves as a social, or human services, agency, while in sixteen states, there is a separate youth corrections agency that oversees this responsibility. In twelve states, delinquency institutions are under the jurisdiction of the adult departments of corrections. Six states place the responsibility in an agency that also offers child protective services (Griffin, 2000). Those youths who are committed to the state juvenile justice system are sent out of the local jurisdiction. Most often, the state agency that administers the juvenile corrections system makes every decision regarding the committed youth. Decisions often include which program the youth will be sentenced, how long the youth will stay, and what treatment will be administered. These decisions are generally made by the state agency and not the local judge (Griffin, 2000).

In most states, juvenile justice relies on larger, secure institutions called training schools or youth centers. However, state run institutions and programs can include reception and diagnostic centers, day treatment centers, shelters, camps, ranches, farms, boot camps and group homes, and also may include training schools or youth centers with various custody level classifications. There may also be placements for youth who have mental health treatment needs (Trojanowicz, Morash and Schram, 2001; Bartollas and Miller, 2001).

Aftercare

Another crucial area of juvenile processing is the aftercare given to juveniles upon release. Aftercare programs refer to treatment given to juveniles after they have been released from a juvenile correctional facility (Light, 1991). Such programs are designed to help juveniles change the underlying behavioral problems that led them to appear before the juvenile court. When aftercare programs are offered, there are conditions associated with receiving these provisions. If juveniles fail to adhere to prescribed conditions, they will be returned to correctional confinement. In most cases, the state agency that oversees the juvenile correctional institutions will also provide aftercare (Griffin, 2000). Some scholars contend that the quality of aftercare provisions that juveniles receive may be contingent upon state resources or the amount of money state agencies allot for this treatment response (Anderson, Burns, and Dyson, 1997). Some criminal justice experts argue that when states experience strain on correctional and juvenile justice budgets, many offenders may not receive the quality aftercare provisions needed to make a successful adjustment to their respective community.

An aftercare program that has gained widespread popularity is called the intensive aftercare program (IAP) which is used for high-risk delinquents. The RAND Corporation has conducted evaluation research on two such programs and found that youths who were placed into intensive supervision groups experienced fewer re-arrests, convictions, and incarceration for new offenses (Sontheimer, Goodstein, and Kovacevic, 1990). Experts warn not to assume that every IAP program will be effective, but rather efforts should be made to determine if other programs will meet with similar success.

ACADEMIC TEACHING POSITIONS

Most academic teaching positions are held by faculty referred to as professors. Professors are responsible for performing many duties that include: (1) transmitting the body of knowledge to undergraduate, as well as graduate students; (2) procuring external funds through grant writing; (3) researching and publishing to contribute to the academic body of knowledge; (4) serving on departmental, college, and university-wide committees; and (5) providing community services to the local and academic community (i.e., reviewing journals and book manuscripts, holding an office in a criminal justice or criminology organization, or participating at conferences). College professors have a nine month contract. Summer teaching is voluntary and is based on the availability of students. Sometimes professors receive a flat rate for each class. Other times, they receive 10% of their contract for each class taught during the summer session. There are several academic teaching ranks that a faculty member can occupy, such as: instructor, adjunct professor, visiting professor, assistant professor, associate professor, professor, distinguished professor, and professor emeritus.

Academic Ranks

Instructors

These teaching positions are usually held by master's and doctoral candidates in order to provide them with teaching experience. Some universities require that, in order to teach, doctoral candidates must have completed all course work in their degree program and have successfully passed the comprehensive examinations. Instructors teach introductory level courses as part of an assistantship or fellowship. In many cases, instructors teach only one course each semester.

Adjunct
Professors

These professors teach on a part-time basis. They are usually persons with full-time jobs and teach evening classes. While they may hold a Ph.D. degree, they typically have a master's degree in criminal justice or criminology or a juris doctorate (law degree).

Visiting
Professors

These professors are normally assistant professors who are A.B.D. (all but dissertation) or have a Ph.D. who accept a nine month teaching assignment. Sometimes these positions are used to attract an individual who will eventually be placed in a tenure tract position. Colleges and universities commonly use them when it is believed that funds eventually will be allocated to open a permanent position. During the process of "visiting," the professor is being evaluated and considered for permanent employment.

| Assistant Professors | These professors can either be A.B.D. or Ph.D. They are typically at this rank when they accept their first teaching position. They could either be tenure track or non-tenure track. They are expected to serve a probationary period of five to six years depending on where they accept employment. |

Assistant
Professors

These professors can either be A.B.D. or Ph.D. They are typically at this rank when they accept their first teaching position. They could either be tenure track or non-tenure track. They are expected to serve a probationary period of five to six years depending on where they accept employment.

Associate
Professors

These professors hold a Ph.D. and have been promoted from the assistant professor rank. This normally occurs after the professor has been actively involved in research, publication, quality teaching, and providing services. Each institution has its own criteria for promotion.

Professors

These professors are Ph.D.s who have been promoted from the associate rank. This normally occurs after the professor has contributed substantially to his or her chosen academic field with grant writing, and publishing of a book manuscript or a significant number of articles. These professors usually have regional reputations. Many professors at Ivy League schools and state-supported universities never attain this rank.

Distinguished
Professor

Few professors ever reach the level of distinguished professor. They are usually scholars with a national and/or international reputation who hold the rank of Professor.

Professor
Emeritus

A professor, who is retired, but is given active status to teach courses on a part-time basis. In more cases than not, the status is an honor and is usually decided from within the department.

WHEN SEARCHING FOR EMPLOYMENT

After the doctoral student finishes his or her program of study and has the status of A.B.D. (all but dissertation. This is not an official academic title.) or Ph.D., he or she typically performs an exhaustive search for a teaching position. del Carmen and Polk (2001) argue that doctoral candidates often lack needed information regarding employment in criminology and criminal justice. Applicants should be aware that they could apply for a tenure track position or a nontenured track position. With a tenure track position, if granted after five or six years, the professor is given a permanent position at his or her respective college or university for a lifetime (few institutions do not allow for lifetime consideration). Nontenure track positions are never permanent and there is no job security. Nontenure track employees can simply be asked to leave at the end of their contract since they serve at the will and pleasure of the department Chair. Despite this, some institutions may allow for promotions of nontenure track positions. As an incentive to remain at an institution, some may allow nontenured faculty to advance from assistant to associate to Professor without ever offering job security.

The idea of having tenure or a lifetime appointment has been questioned recently. Some institutions (very few in number) are eliminating tenure altogether and providing other incentives for professors to remain on the job. For example, Jacobson (2002) reports that some institutions are providing professors with an option to either apply for tenure after their probationary period if they are tenure track, or sign a five year renewable contract that would pay an extra 15 percent increase in salary. Some professors are opting for the money instead of the long-term security.

CHOOSING THE CORRECT COLLEGE OR UNIVERSITY

While searching for a teaching position, the applicant will also discover that there are several types of academic institutions where he or she may seek employment: Ivy League schools, state universities, regional schools, and community colleges. The applicant should be aware that the initial selection could determine future options and mobility. For example, if one selects an institution that emphasizes teaching and he or she spends several years there and never publishes because it is not required to receive tenure or a promotion, it may be difficult to attain employment at a research institution, because there is no publication track record.

Ivy League schools are prestigious and extremely competitive. They are considered research institutions. They primarily emphasize grant writing followed by quality publications of book manuscripts and articles in top tier, peer reviewed journals. Hirees are typically those with national and international reputations. These schools are primarily concerned with the dissemination of scholarship. Teaching is important, but is second to research. They are also concerned with community service. Applicants must be aware of the demands required by such schools as part of the tenure track position. These positions are very difficult to acquire since many Ivy League schools lack criminal justice and criminology programs.

Most state-supported universities, especially the larger ones, are competitive. They too are considered research institutions. Hirees are expected to write grants, publish articles in top tier peer reviewed journals and demonstrate quality teaching and community services. Those who are tenured track are often given a three-year evaluation and apply for tenure during their fifth year. In most cases, they are expected to publish one or two articles each year from the start of employment. They are required to teach a minimum of six hours or two courses. They are allowed reduced teaching loads, because of the time needed to do research.

Regional schools emphasize teaching, publishing, grant writing, and community service. The teaching load is usually 12 hours, or four courses each semester. Because professors spend so much time teaching, these schools tend to accept both peer and non-peer reviewed articles published in either tier journals to be used towards tenure. At most regional schools, professors can be tenured after five years of service.

Community colleges emphasize teaching, community service, and publications. Grant writing is rarely emphasized. The teaching load is usually 15 hours, or five courses each semester. However, unlike fourr-year institutions, professors at community colleges can be awarded tenure and advance through the ranks with a master's degree.

A proper understanding of the main emphasis of each college or university should allow the respective applicant to make an informed decision about where to seek employment. For example, if one is not partial to publishing or grant writing, he or she would probably not want to seek employment at a "publish or perish" institution. Those who enjoy teaching should probably target a college or university that emphasizes teaching rather than research. However, doctoral students with grant writing experience and a number of publications may feel drawn to highly competitive environments.

CHOOSING THE CORRECT GEOGRAPHICAL AREA

Professors often complain about the climate and culture surrounding their institution. While interviewing for a teaching position, the applicant can avoid this problem by targeting a desired area. For example, if the applicant is from a warm or hot region of the country, he or she might have a difficult time transitioning to a cold, snowy, and icy environment. At the same time, if one is leaving a school located in an urban area to take employment in a rural area, it may be problematic to become acclimated to an area that lacks multiculturalism and an abundance of social activities. The new hiree may experience culture shock and suffer needlessly. These two issues alone can be very important and could exacerbate stress and cause disappointment. Moreover, if the applicant has a family, he or she should consider the prospect of employment opportunities for the trailing spouse and the quality of the state's educational system for their children. In essence, the applicant should consider the quality of life that the new area has to offer along with its health care system.

ON INTERVIEWING: SOME BASIC SUGGESTIONS

After the prospective candidate has submitted a cover letter, curriculum vitae, and names of references (in response to a teaching vacancy), he or she may be contacted to arrange an interview. The interview signals to a potential candidate that a college is interested in offering employment. If the institution fails to respond or offer an interview to a prospective candidate, it usually means that the institution has no interest in offering employment or the advertised position may have been contingent upon the availability of funds that were never given to the department. However, in most cases, the applicant will receive a courtesy letter thanking him or her for expressing interest in the institution. When an interview is granted, it is considered the most important part of the application process, because the negotiation can be made or lost if the interview does not go smoothly. There are several important things that the applicant should do:

- The applicant should remember that the interview begins when he or she "gets off" the plane and it ends when one "gets back" on the plane. Essentially, faculty members evaluate the interviewee at the time that he or she is picked up at the airport until the person is returned to the airport. The candidate should be aware that several other candidates will be interviewed for the same position. The applicant must be aware that his or her demeanor and mannerisms are being observed and scrutinized. Therefore, one should be on his or her best behavior for the duration of the interview.

- The institution and/or department should make all visiting arrangements including flight reservations, hotel, and defray the cost of meals. The department should also provide an itinerary to the applicant. Sometimes doctoral fellows are unaware that the institution and/or department that grants them the interview is responsible for defraying the cost of their flight, hotel, and food. However, when it is not clearly stated by the institution/ department, the interviewee should inquire about who will pay for the interview. It is not uncommon for some institutions and/or departments to require the interviewee to make initial payments and reimburse the candidate afterwards. Before going on an interview, the candidate should make sure that he or she gets an itinerary from the host college to learn of the expectations. For example, an itinerary will usually include the events in which the candidate will participate during the visit. One would probably want to know how much time that he or she must devote to a presentation.

- The candidate should always dress professionally. Men should wear a dark suit and tie. Women should wear a dark business suit or dress. Women should also wear simple jewelry and light make-up. The male and female candidate should avoid strong fragrance, multiple piercings, and exposing tattoos. The candidate should remember that first impressions are lasting ones. One should not wear a tee shirt, shorts, and tennis shoes nor should women wear open toe shoes. A department's faculty might take offense to this kind of behavior believing the candidate lacks professionalism and maturity.

- The candidate should always respect their future colleagues. During the interview, the candidate should always remember to address them by their professional title or rank. This exhibition of respect may be a point that will win over many potential colleagues.

- The candidate should be prepared to answer a commonly asked question, how does our department benefit from hiring you? This question requires that the candidate research the department where he or she is seeking employment. It requires that the candidate know the strengths and weaknesses of the department and how he or she can actually help to improve the department or at least be a good fit.

- The applicant should find out if he or she is expected to teach a class as part of the visit and ask what subject matter is desired as part of the interview. Most institutions desire to see the potential hire in action. As part of the interview, departments will arrange so that the interviewee will teach at least one class. In most cases, it is a very short class. Most departments seek to measure how well a new hire interacts with students. For candidates desperately seeking employment, this could be an extremely stressful experience. One way to minimize the stress is to ask beforehand how much time should be devoted to teaching and what subject matter is preferred as a general topic. This helps the potential hire to relax and practice before the big performance.

- The candidate should be able to articulate a research agenda for the next couple of years. Many institutions/departments are concerned about faculty productivity. Because of this, many are concerned if new hires will be productive as a new faculty member. As such, one can expect to be questioned about his or her future research agenda. At the same time, it could lead to collaborative research with faculty members who have similar research interests.

- The candidate should be able to expound upon his or her teaching philosophy. In many cases, departments that are not diversified may or may not be interested in hiring a new faculty with a similar teaching philosophy. For example, in most criminal justice and criminology departments, the teaching philosophy is a conservative one. The question that should emerge is to what extent are such departments looking for someone who offers a liberal or radical orientation. This is not to suggest that there is something inherently wrong about having such teaching philosophies, but the candidate would do well to know the general teaching philosophy of the department in which he or she is seeking employment.

- The candidate must be aware that in a social setting, such as dinner, he or she should not drink or smoke excessively even if others do. The applicant has to remember that he or she is the center of attention and the reason why everyone is congregating. At the same time, if the candidate has been extremely impressive in the classroom all could be lost if it is sensed by the interviewer(s) that the candidate has a drinking problem. A strong performance can be negated by poor character or judgement. The candidate must remember that the job is not his or hers until an offer is made. The applicant must remember that the interview is not completed until he or she gets back on the plane.

- If making a lateral move, the candidate should not make negative remarks about current colleagues. One does not know if future colleagues know your current colleagues. Gossiping may give others the impression that you're not collegial. When leaving a job to accept a new position, the candidate must remember that the academic community is not as large as it may seem and many within the community know each other. As such, proper decorum is essential. For example, while interviewing for a new position, the applicant should never reveal damaging or disparaging information about his or her colleagues. This could signal to new colleagues that the applicant is not very collegial or that he or she could be a busy body. With this, the possibility exists for the potential hire to cause disruption or friction in the newly desired department.

- The candidate should remember only to ask questions of a department faculty when they ask if you have questions. Remember, this interview is about them getting to know you. The faculty should never be made to feel as if they are interviewing for a new job. The interviewee should realize that the interview is the appropriate time for a new faculty to get to know him or her.

- The interviewee should be familiar with new colleagues' research and teaching interests. As part of the interviewee's research, he or she should make at least a cursory examination of the research literature to have an idea about the research interests of new colleagues. This could prove impressive and beneficial during the interview.

- The candidate will meet separately with each faculty member. If he or she feels comfortable with the professors, he or she may ask about how the tenure process worked in the past to gauge whether it's fair. If it is not, this could signal problems ahead. This approach to finding out much needed information might be less intimidating than asking a department Chair or Vice-President about salary increases, promotion and tenure.

- While at the hotel, the candidate should watch the local news and read the local newspaper to discover if the city, county, and state are having problems. Candidates will find that most faculty members are reluctant to make negative comments about their institution, city, and state. A candidate could unknowingly be entering a negative situation. One could receive reports on the status of an institution or the state's budget that is being allocated to the higher education system. One could also learn of problems that an institution may be facing. Such information could help the candidate make an informed decision if the position is offered.

- It does not hurt to leave the hotel and tour parts of the city that your host has neglected to show. The institution could be in a high crime area. During an interview, one is rarely told about the quality of life of the community that surrounds the institution. Faculty rarely discuss the locations of hospitals, local schools, grocery stores, or fire and police departments. To some, especially those with a family, this is invaluable information that will weigh heavily in their decision to either accept or reject employment if a position is offered. The candidate would do well to leave his or her hotel during the evening hours to explore the city and surrounding areas to discover if the environment is safe or whether it is dangerous. The candidate should remember that if the department is seeking you, members would never say anything to give the candidate a negative impression of the institution.

- Above all, the candidate should never discuss salary until the position is offered. The candidate should know if the college is interested in hiring him or her because usually after the interview, the job will be offered. At that point, it is considered proper to discuss a salary or even negotiate an acceptable salary.

- If the position is offered, ask for several weeks to consider the offer. In most cases, institutions/departments will allow the candidate a couple of weeks to provide them with a decision. This is considered proper because if the candidate refuses, the institution/department has additional time to seek another faculty for hire.

- Send well-prepared, legible, handwritten thank you notes immediately upon your return home. The note should be sent to the chair of the search committee and to the chair of the department.

NEGOTIATING THE DEAL

- If one of your objectives is to have security, the applicant should make sure the position is tenure track. Most professors usually seek a position that is tenure track because it brings job security. In most cases, after a professor has been employed at a university for five years, he or she typically applies for tenure. Tenure is usually awarded if the applicant has made accomplishments in the areas of teaching, scholarship, and community service. Tenure brings security in that professors are rarely terminated from employment after tenure is awarded. However, tenure can be lost under unusual circumstances. Currently, some institutions are experimenting with eliminating tenure and yet other institutions have implemented a post-tenure review process. The purpose of the latter is to ensure that professors remain productive, the former is to eliminate the monies that universities will have to spend in the long run for professors who become marginal.

- When the position is offered, the candidate should ask for a fair salary — find out what others in the same department are making (it is public information at state-supported institutions). Doctoral fellows are usually unaware about what is an appropriate salary when seeking a teaching position. For some, this may cause stress when interviewing for employment. One easy way to reduce the anxiety over what is an appropriate salary is to ask one's mentor or the Chair of the department where one is interviewing.

- If possible, the applicant should attempt to negotiate the number of courses he or she will teach, (one could argue that you need release time for research). After graduating from a doctoral program or leaving a teaching position, the candidate should attempt to negotiate the number of courses he or she will teach. While teaching is good, a doctoral degree is a research degree. Professors are expected to engage in extensive research by trying to procure grants and writing scholarly material for publications. Professors should not only teach and perform community service, but they must also contribute to the body of knowledge for their respective disciplines. In doing so, it increases the likelihood of promotion and tenure. It also increases mobility if the professor chooses to make a lateral move to another college or university.

- The candidate should ask for a computer, printer, software, and other needed items. For faculty who are committed to research and publication, it is essential that they have the tools and equipment needed to engage in research. For example, those who engage in quantitative research need statistical applications to analyze data. If they are active in writing and submitting manuscripts for publication consideration, they will need to have a computer and printer.

- The candidate should ask for relocation or moving expenses. After the candidate has agreed to accept a position, it may require him or her to relocate to another city or state. When this occurs, it may require hiring a moving company to literally pack and load one's entire apartment or house and move and unload every item to the new location. The new faculty should contact a number of movers to get the best estimate, the estimate should quickly be given to the new employer so that it can either be accepted or rejected. The process is commonly used since institutions may place limits on the amount given for moving and relocating expenses. In some cases, the newly hired may have to pay for the cost and later be reimbursed. The candidate should have the amount of the moving allowance stated in the contract.

- The candidate should ask for start-up funds (usually $5,000 at many larger institutions). Start-up money is used for purchasing tools and equipment needed to get the newly hired off to a good start in the new position. In most cases, money may be allocated for computers, software, trips, and other materials needed for the faculty member to engage in research. The newly hired should also monitor the amount of money that he or she spends and have it stated that the money is to roll over the following year if it is not exhausted during the first year of employment.

- The candidate should ask if the department supports visits to the American Society of Criminology (ASC) and the Academy of Criminal Justice Sciences (ACJS) conferences. It is important that faculty members (especially the newly hired) attend the major conferences of their respective disciplines. By attending conferences, faculty are essentially advertising for their university. They advertise to undergraduate and other graduate students who may be undecided about where to matriculate for their graduate education. At the same time, faculty advertise to other professors and researchers with the hope that it will lead to collaborative research with those having similar research interests.

- The candidate should ask if the institution offers college tuition support (usually called tuition waivers) for their children. Some universities will allow the children of employees to either attend the university free or attend at a drastically reduced cost. For example, some universities will defray 80 to 90 percent of the cost. In some rare cases, such as with Vanderbilt University, it pays up to 90 percent if children of its employees attend any college in Tennessee, and 75 percent if they attend anywhere else in the country.

- The candidate should ask how often faculty are given salary increases. Since many states are facing cutbacks because of the economy, institutions across the country are facing tough economic times. Some institutions have implemented across the board hiring freezes and others have simply opted for not giving raises to employees. Despite this, some institutions and departments may have special funds set aside for merit raises given to those with superior scholastic performances. These colleges may represent the exception rather than the rule. The newly hired may want to inquire about this area. He or she may discover that employees may not have received a salary increase in quite some time. This information may be of more interest to faculty with children or those who desire to purchase a home or other property.

- If interested, the candidate should ask whether summer teaching is a possibility. At most institutions, summer teaching is not guaranteed because it is based on the availability of students who enroll for summer courses. At some institutions, preferential treatment may be given to senior professors and at other schools, senior professors and researchers usually take the summer off to either vacation or pursue research interests. Many professors use the summer as an opportunity to supplement or increase their salary. For example, some institutions have different pay scales during the summer. Some may offer the faculty a flat rate for each course while others may pay a percentage of the professor's contract for summer teaching.

- The candidate should have the contract in hand before moving. In a small number of cases, it has been reported by some that agreement terms (salary, office space, computer and printer, number of classes, etc.) were not properly secured upon their arrival to their new job. When this occurs, a lack of evidence in the form of a contract places the newly hired at the mercy of the institution for at least an academic year. In order to avoid a potentially negative situation, the newly hired should get a contract in hand before relocating to the institution chosen for employment.

LATERAL MOVES

Professors may choose to leave an institution for a number of reasons that could range from the desire to pursue greater opportunities, challenge, growth, and a higher salary to failure to receive promotion or tenure. When the decision to leave one position for another is finalized, the professor should do the following when applying for a new position:

- The candidate should ask for the same rank and never accept a lower rank or reduced salary unless there are compelling reasons. When a professor has earned the rank or status of associate professor, it usually means that he or she has spent at least five years as an assistant professor. In most cases, the increase in rank brings an increase in salary. When making a lateral move, the faculty member should keep this point in mind. The reality is that associate professors are paid more than others below this rank. One would be hard pressed to take a reduced rank and a reduced salary after reaching the associate level status unless compelling reasons exist to justify such an unusual course of action.

- The candidate should ask for a salary that is equal to what others are earning who hold the same rank (research the low, middle, and high ranges). The newly hired can ask the department's Chair the candid question of how much professors in the department are making, or one could go to the university library to ascertain this information, or visit www.salary.com to get an idea of what the salary scale is like at the institution.

- If the candidate is tenured, he or she should ask that tenure be a part of the contract. (If the request is denied, ask to apply for tenure at the end of the first year to be granted during/for the hired eligibility after a few years. Some will allow it after the first year, but the rule is to allow it after three years. Institutions are concerned with whether newly hired are still committed to research and productivity. The newly hired should get the agreement in writing as part of the contract. A failure to do so could mean that the professor will have to wait an additional five years before being eligible for tenure, despite having received it at his or her previous institution.

- The candidate should try to negotiate a reduced teaching load, if possible. Some departments allow certain faculty to have a reduced teaching load. In most cases, this is based on factors such as time needed to conduct research and publish scholarly materials.

- The candidate should ask for a computer, printer, software, and other needed equipment. The time to ask for tools and equipment is at the interview stage of the hiring process. This is one of the times when departments are more generous to a professor they would like to hire. In fact, one should have these items listed as part of the contract. Failure to do so could mean that the new faculty member will not have new equipment or any equipment at all.

- The candidate should ask for relocation or moving expenses. After the candidate has agreed to accept a position, it may require him or her to relocate to another city or state. When this occurs, it may require hiring a moving company to literally pack and load one's entire apartment or house, move, and unload every item at the new location. The new faculty member should contact a number of movers to get the best estimate, and the estimate should quickly be given to the new employer so that it can either be accepted or rejected. The process is commonly used since institutions may place limits on the amount given for moving and relocating expenses. In some cases, the newly hired may have to pay for the cost of moving and later be reimbursed. The candidate should have the amount of the moving allowance stated in the contract.

- The candidate should ask for start-up funds (usually $5,000 at many larger institutions). Start-up money is used for purchasing tools and equipment needed to get the newly hired off to a good start in the new position. In most cases, money may be allocated for computers, software, trips, and other materials needed for the faculty member to engage in research. The newly hired should also monitor the amount of money that he or she spends and have it stated that the money is to roll over the following year if it is not exhausted during the first year of employment.

- If there is a trailing spouse (in academia), the candidate should ask the institution to offer his or her spouse employment or at least assist in finding employment (since most state-supported institutions have various versions of the nepotism law). Spouse employment may be easier to accomplish when both are in the same field of study. The process becomes more difficult, if not impossible, when the two are in different disciplines. The problem arises because a Chair has no influence on the hiring decisions of another department. However, the Dean could intervene and use his or her influence to hire the trailing spouse. When possible, it should be stated in the contract.

- If a candidate is interviewed, offered, and accepts a new position, he or she should get the new contract in hand before resigning from the current place of employment. The contract is legally binding and serves to ensure that any agreement made as a condition of employment must be honored. The contract is legally binding in court.

When searching for an academic teaching or administrative position, the prospective employee should first search the following employment web sites:

A.   The Chronicle of Higher Education at www.chronicle.com/jobs/
B.   The American Society of Criminology at www.asc41.com
C.   Academy of Criminal Justice Sciences at www.acjs.com
D.   HigherEdJobs.com

As an applicant who has been granted an interview, one should not worry because the interview is hardly ever granted to anyone unless there is something impressive in his or her vita. In most cases, there is a real possibility that you will be hired unless something is done during the interview to give the interviewer(s) the impression that the candidate is not suited for the position, or is not a good match for the department and/or the institution. Institutions will not needlessly spend money flying a candidate to their city, and providing lodging and meals for several days if they do not intend to hire him or her. So applicants try to relax.

SOME SELECTED INSTITUTIONS TO CONSIDER FOR EMPLOYMENT

Today, it is estimated that there are over 1,200 criminal justice/ criminology programs in the United States. As a result, there exists enormous employment potential for those seeking careers as criminal justice educators. While this is not an exhaustive list, the authors have tried to target some criminal justice and criminology programs in every state in the U.S. and designate them as research or teaching departments and provide the types of degrees they offer so that applicants can make a more informed decision regarding future employment.

STATE and SCHOOL	TYPE OF DEPT.	BS	MS	DEGREE JD/Ph.D.
Alabama				
Alabama State University	Teaching	x	x	
Auburn University at Montgomery	Research	x	x	
Troy State University	Research	x	x	
Uni. of Alabama - Tuscaloosa	Research	x	x	
Uni. of Alabama - Birmingham	Research	x	x	
Uni. of South Alabama	Teaching	x		
Alaska				
University of Alaska - Anchorage	Research	x	x	
University of Alaska - Fairbanks	Research	x	x	
Arizona				
Apache University	Research	x	x	
Arizona State University	Research	x	x	Joint
Northern Arizona University	Research	x	x	

Arkansas

University of Arkansas - Little Rock	Research	x	x	
University of Arkansas - Pine Bluff	Teaching	x		

California

California State University - Fresno	Research	x	x	
California State University - Long Beach	Research	x	x	
California State University - Sacramento	Research	x	x	
California State Univ. - San Bernardino	Research	x	x	
Sonoma State University	Research	x	x	
University of California - Irvine	Research	x	x	x

Colorado

University of Colorado	Research	x	x
University of Colorado - Denver	Research	x	x
University of Denver	Research	x	x

Connecticut

Central Connecticut State University	Research	x	x
Western Connecticut State University	Research	x	x

Delaware

University of Delaware	Research	x	x	x

District of Columbia

American University	Research	x	x
George Washington University	Research	x	x

Florida

Florida Atlantic University	Research	x	x	
Florida State University	Research	x	x	x
University of Central Florida	Research	x	x	
University of North Florida	Research	x	x	
University of South Florida	Research	x	x	x

Georgia

Albany State University	Teaching	x	x
Armstrong Atlantic State University	Teaching	x	x
Clark-Atlanta State University	Teaching	x	x
Georgia State University	Research	x	x
Valdosta State University	Teaching	x	x

Hawaii

Chaminade University in Honolulu	Research	x	x
University of Hawaii at Hilo	Teaching	x	

Idaho

Boise State University	Research	x	x
Lewis-Clark State University	Teaching	x	x
University of Idaho	Teaching	x	

Illinois

Chicago State University	Teaching	x	x	
Illinois State University	Research	x	x	
Northern Illinois State University	Research	x	x	
Southern Illinois University - Carbondale	Research	x	x	
University of Illinois at Chicago	Research	x	x	x
Western Illinois University	Research	x	x	

Indiana

Indiana University - Bloomington	Research	x	x	x
Indiana Uni. Purdue Uni. - Indianapolis	Research	x	x	
Indiana University Northwest	Research	x	x	
Indiana State University	Research	x	x	

Iowa

Buena Vista University	Teaching	x	
St. Ambrose University	Teaching	x	x
Upper Iowa University	Teaching	x	
University of Northern Iowa	Teaching	x	

Kansas

Wasburn University	Teaching	x	
Wichita State University	Research	x	x

Kentucky

Eastern Kentucky University	Research	x	x
Morehead State University	Teaching	x	x
University of Louisville	Research	x	x

Louisiana

Grambling State University	Teaching	x	x
Northeast Louisiana University	Teaching	x	x
Southern University at New Orleans	Teaching	x	x
St. John's University	Teaching	x	x
University of Louisiana at Monroe	Teaching	x	x

Maine

Southern Maine University	Teaching	x
University of Maine - Presque Isle	Teaching	x

Maryland

Coppin State University	Teaching	x	x	
University of Baltimore	Research	x	x	
University of Maryland - College Park	Research	x	x	x
University of Maryland - Eastern Shore	Teaching	x	x	

Massachusetts

Northeastern University	Research	x	x	
Suffolk University	Research	x	x	
University of Massachusetts - Amherst	Teaching	x		
University of Massachusetts - Boston	Teaching	x		
University of Massachusetts - Lowell	Research	x	x	
Westfield State College	Teaching	x	x	

Michigan

Eastern Michigan University	Research	x	x	
Ferris State University	Research	x	x	
Grand Valley State University	Teaching	x	x	
Michigan State University	Research	x	x	x
Northern Michigan University	Research	x	x	

Minnesota

Bemidji State University	Teaching	x	x	
Minnesota State University - Mankato	Teaching	x		
Minnesota State University - Moorhead	Teaching	x		
St. Cloud State University	Teaching	x	x	

Mississippi

Delta State University	Teaching	x		
Mississippi College	Teaching	x	x	
Mississippi Valley State University	Teaching	x		
University of Southern Mississippi	Research	x	x	x

Missouri

Central Missouri State University	Teaching	x	x	
Drury University	Teaching	x	x	
University of Missouri - Kansas City	Research	x	x	
University of Missouri - St. Louis	Research	x	x	x
Southeast Missouri State University	Teaching	x	x	

Nebraska

University of Nebraska - Kearney	Research	x	x	
University of Nebraska - Lincoln	Research	x	x	x
University of Nebraska - Omaha	Research	x	x	x

Nevada

University of Nevada - Las Vegas	Research	x	x	
University of Nevada - Reno	Teaching	x		

New Jersey

New Jersey City University	Teaching	x	x	
Rutgers University - Camden	Research	x	x	
Rutgers University - Newark	Research	x	x	x
Seton Hall University	Teaching	x		

New Mexico

Eastern New Mexico University	Teaching	x		
New Mexico State University	Research	x	x	

New York

Albany State University	Research	x	x	x
Buffalo State University	Research	x	x	
Iona College	Research	x	x	
John Jay College	Research	x	x	x
Long Island University - Brentwood	Research	x	x	
Long Island University - C.W. Post	Research	x	x	
Niagara University	Research	x	x	
State University of New York - Albany	Research	x	x	x
State University of New York - Buffalo	Research	x	x	

North Carolina

Appalachian State University	Teaching	x	x	
East Carolina University	Research	x	x	
North Carolina Central University	Teaching	x	x	
University of North Carolina - Charlotte	Teaching	x	x	
University of North Carolina - Greensboro	Teaching	x	x	

North Dakota

Minot State University	Teaching	x	x	
University of North Dakota	Teaching	x		

Ohio

Bowling Green State University	Research	x	x	
Kent State University	Research	x	x	
Tiffin University	Research	x	x	
University of Cincinnati	Research	x	x	x
Xavier University	Research	x	x	
Youngstown State University	Teaching	x	x	

Oklahoma

East Central University	Teaching	x	x	
Northwestern State University	Teaching	x	x	
University of Central Oklahoma	Teaching	x	x	

Oregon

Portland State University	Research	x	x	
Western Oregon University	Research	x	x	

Pennsylvania

California University of Pennsylvania	Research	x	x	
Indiana University - Pennsylvania	Research	x	x	x
Mercyhurst College	Research	x	x	
Pennsylvania State Uni. - Harrisburg	Research	x	x	
Pennsylvania State Uni. - University Park	Research	x	x	x
Shippensburg University	Research	x	x	
Saint Joseph's University	Research	x	x	
Temple University	Research	x	x	x
Villanova University	Research	x	x	

Rhode Island

Roger Williams University	Research	x	x	
Salve Regina University	Teaching	x	x	

South Carolina

The Citadel	Teaching	x		
University of South Carolina - Columbia	Research	x	x	

Tennessee

East Tennessee State University	Teaching	x	x	
Middle Tennessee State University	Teaching	x	x	
Tennessee State University	Teaching	x	x	
University of Memphis	Teaching	x	x	
University of Tennessee - Chattanooga	Teaching	x	x	

Texas

St. Mary's University	Research	x	x	
Sam Houston State University	Research	x	x	Joint
Southwest Texas State University	Teaching	x	x	
Sul Ross State University	Teaching	x	x	
Tarleton State Uni. - Central Texas	Teaching	x	x	
University of North Texas	Research	x	x	
University of Texas - Arlington	Research	x	x	
University of Texas - Austin	Research	x	x	
University of Texas - San Antonio	Research	x	x	

Utah

Weber State University	Research	x	x

Virginia

George Mason University	Research	x	
Radford University	Research	x	x
University of Richmond	Research	x	x
Virginia Commonwealth University	Research	x	x
Virginia State University	Teaching	x	
Virginia Union University	Teaching	x	

Washington

Gonzaga University	Teaching	x	
Washington State University	Research	x	x

West Virginia

Marshall University	Teaching	x	x
West Virginia State College	Teaching	x	

Wisconsin

Marquette University	Research	x	x
University of Wisconsin - LaCrosse	Teaching	x	
University of Wisconsin - Milwaukee	Research	x	x
University of Wisconsin - Parkside	Teaching	x	
University of Wisconsin - Stout	Teaching	x	

RESEARCH POSITIONS

After some students complete their doctoral program, instead of pursuing a career as a criminal justice educator, they may choose employment at a research agency. In most cases, these are doctoral students who discover early that they do not desire to make teaching a career. They are typically those who enjoy conducting research and not standing in front of a class lecturing. Other times, professors who are disenchanted with teaching and the tenure process, may seek a career change and research may present itself as a viable option. When the decision is made, the applicant could seek employment as a researcher with either of the following: (1) the RAND Corporation; (2) National Institute of Justice (NIJ); (3) Vera Institute of Justice; (4) a post-doctoral fellow at the National Consortium of Violence Research (NCOVR); (5) Police Executive Research Forum (PERF); or (6) the American Bar Foundation (ABF).

RAND Corporation

RAND was created in 1946 as a "think tank." It provides an intellectual environment that assists all branches of the U.S. military, as well as seek viable policy solutions for social and international issues. RAND is a nonprofit institution that helps to improve policy and decision-making through research and analysis. It strives to develop knowledge to inform decision-makers without suggesting any specific course of action. In the area of criminal justice, RAND seeks criminologists and social scientists to conduct research and analysis. More specifically, RAND's Division of Safety and Justice seeks mid- to senior-level researchers interested in crime, delinquency, and public safety. RAND provides opportunities to collaborate with outside organizations and research partners, as well as to work on the local, state, and national levels.

RAND's Public Safety and Justice researchers must use both quantitative and qualitative methodologies. They work in multidisciplinary teams. Researchers examine a variety of issues, including sentencing and corrections, youth violence and prevention development, drug policy and community violence. The research positions require a Ph.D. in criminology, sociology, or related social science and a minimum number of years. RAND has four principal locations, Santa Monica, California; Arlington, Virginia; Pittsburgh, Pennsylvania; and RAND Europe. RAND is also headquartered in the Netherlands, Berlin, Germany and Cambridge and the United Kingdom. RAND disseminates its research findings to local, state and federal governments.

National Institute of Justice

The National Institute of Justice (NIJ) is the research and development agency of the U.S. Department of Justice that is solely devoted to researching crime control and justice-related issues. Its authority is derived from the Omnibus Crime Control and Safe Streets Act of 1968. NIJ provides objective, independent, non-partisan, evidence-based knowledge and tools of crime and justice at the state and local levels.

NIJ's primary goals are to prevent and reduce crime, improve law enforcement and the administration of justice, and promote public safety. The Office of Research and Evaluation at NIJ develops, conducts, directs and supervises comprehensive research and evaluation activities through two integrated vehicles: (1) extramural research, which involves outside researchers who often collaborate with criminal justice practitioners, and (2) intramural research conducted by office staff. Research and evaluation cut across an array of topics that are found within the institute's charter. Some areas include violence, drug abuse, criminal behavior, organized crime, gangs, corrections, prosecution, sentencing, victimization, policing, drug testing, crime prevention, and crime mapping. The Office of Research and Evaluation identifies and prioritizes issues and builds knowledge that informs policymakers, practitioners, researchers, and the public. NIJ seeks Social Science Analysts and Senior Social Science Analysts for research. Those who typically work in the Office of Research and Evaluation have a Ph.D. in criminal justice, criminology, statistics and methods, or other areas of the social sciences.

Vera Institute of Justice

The Vera Institute is a nonprofit organization that emerged as a reaction to the injustice of the New York bail system that granted release based on income. The Vera Foundation was created to discover ways to make the system fair. The result was Vera demonstrated that poor New Yorkers with strong ties to the community could be safely released before trial. Vera essentially created a successful alternative to bail called release on recognizance (ROR). As a result, Vera created a nonprofit organization to screen everyone who is arrested and detained. In 1966, the Ford Foundation helped transform the Vera Foundation into the Vera Institute of Justice. Today, Vera develops unexpected, yet practical and affordable solutions to problems in criminal justice (i.e., crime and victimization, policing, the judicial process, sentencing and corrections, and institutions of youth) to make the system fair, humane, and efficient for everyone. Vera often creates nonprofit organizations that study social problems and current responses, and provides advice and assistance needed to change systemic problems.

The Vera Institute hires researchers (senior research associates) with a Ph.D. in criminal justice, criminology, and other areas of social sciences with research experience. Researchers are expected to perform program evaluation; write grants; write research reports; engage in quantitative methodology; visit site projects; work with data; attend conferences; develop demonstration programs; and partner with governmental agencies.

National Consortium on Violence Research

The National Consortium on Violence Research (NCOVR) is a research and training center that specializes in violence research. It was founded in 1995 with a $12 million grant from the National Science Foundation in cooperation with the Department of Housing and Urban

Development (HUD) and NIJ. NCOVR's mission is threefold: (1) to advance basic scientific knowledge about the causes or factors that contribute to interpersonal violence; (2) to train the next generation of violence researchers; and (3) to disseminate its research findings to participants, policymakers, and practitioners.

NCOVR is a multidisciplinary research institution with members from different disciplinary backgrounds, including the social, biological, medical, legal, and political sciences. The consortium offers training to pre- and post-doctoral fellows. Trainees are selected from several disciplines. The fellowships support post-doctoral recipients for up to two years. Pre-doctoral recipients are supported for up to three years. Funds are provided for fellows to attend professional meetings, meet their mentors, and cover out of pocket research costs. NCOVR is headquartered at the H. John Heinz III School of Public Policy and Management at Carnegie Mellon University.

Police Executive Research Forum

Founded in 1977, the Police Executive Research Forum (PERF) is a national organization for progressive police executives from the largest city, county and state law enforcement agencies. PERF's primary goals are to improve policing and advance professionalism through research involvement in public policy debate. PERF members understand the problems associated with leadership in policing. As a result, they work to professionalize policing at all levels by engaging in research, experimentation, and exchanging ideas through public discussions and debates to share knowledge about policing. Members believe that academic study is a prerequisite for acquiring, understanding, and adding to the body of knowledge of professional police management. PERF strives to (1) improve the delivery of police services and crime control nationwide; (2) encourage debate of police and criminal justice issues with the law enforcement community; (3) implement and promote law enforcement research; and (4) provide national leadership, technical assistance and management services to police agencies. PERF receives its operating revenues from government grants and contracts, and partners with private foundations and other organizations. PERF seeks employees with a Ph.D. in criminal justice, criminology, or other social sciences.

American Bar Foundation

The American Bar Foundation (ABF) is an independent research institute that pursues experimental studies of law and legal institutions.

The ABF seeks qualified scholars to join its community of resident research fellows. It seeks full-time junior and senior scholars. Junior fellows must demonstrate outstanding potential while senior scholars must be able to demonstrate outstanding scholarship. ABF fellows initiate, develop, conduct, and publish their own and collaborative scholarly research funded through the ABF's own financial resources or through grants made to individual projects by government agencies and private foundations. The Foundation also provides extensive support services, including research assistance and technical support. Research fellows are provided access to libraries and computer facilities at Northwestern University and the University of Chicago. Fellows at ABF are currently engaged in applied empirical research and normative theory undertaken from a variety of disciplinary and interdisciplinary perspectives. Salaries and fringe benefits are competitive with those at leading research universities. Research fellows must hold a Ph.D. in any social science or possess a law degree.

CONSULTANCIES

Professors and researchers who hold a Ph.D. in criminal justice or criminology may be offered the opportunity to consult. As consultants, professionals are hired to give expert opinion about criminal justice-related issues. This typically occurs within the context of a criminal or civil trial. The expert may be hired to convince a judge or jury about the innocence or guilt of a defendant. One interesting note worth mentioning is that during a criminal trial, both the prosecution and the defense will hire a number of experts to influence the verdict. Some consultants may be experts in the areas of DNA, forensic science, and crime scene investigation. A consultancy may be offered to scholars who are considered experts in their respective areas. In most cases, this occurs when the consultant has written extensively in a particular area. For example, if a criminal justice professor has published books and several articles on the police use of excessive force and is frequently contacted by local media for an expert opinion when police are accused of engaging in the behavior, he or she may be contacted by local or regional lawyers to provide expert opinion when a case goes to trial. The likelihood of acquiring a consultancy is increased if the expert has a regional or national reputation as being one of the best in his or her chosen profession. He or she may be hired to offer an expert opinion that could determine the outcome of a case. Consultants are sometimes paid lucratively for their time and opinions. It is, however, unlikely that a professor or researcher can make a career from consulting alone. Consulting is used to supplement one's income.

REFERENCES

Anderson, J. F., Burns, J., and Dyson, L. (1997). "Effective Aftercare Provisions Could Hold the Key to the Rehabilitative Effects of Shock Incarceration Programs." The Journal of Offender Monitoring. 10(3):10-17.

Anderson, J. F., and Dyson, L. (2001). Legal Rights of Prisoners: Cases and Comments. Landham, MD: University Press of America.

Bartollas and Miller. (2001). Juvenile Justice in America. (3rd ed.). Upper Saddle River, NJ: Prentice Hall Publishing.

Belknap, J. (1984). "The effect of local policy on the sentencing patterns of state wards." Justice Quarterly, 1:549-561.

Coffey, A. R. (1972). Juvenile Justice as a System: Law Enforcement to Rehabilitation. Englewood Cliffs, N.J.: Prentice-Hall.

Cole, G. F. (1995). The American System of Criminal Justice. (7th ed.). Belmont, CA: Wadsworth Publishing Company.

Cole, G. F., and Smith, C. E. (1998). The American System of Criminal Justice. (8th ed.). Belmont, CA: Wadsworth Publishing.

Dannefer, D., and Schutt, R. K. (1982). "Race and juvenile justice processing in court and police agencies." American Journal of Sociology, 87:1113-1132.

del Carmen, A., and Polk, O. E. (2001). Faculty Employment in Criminology and Criminal Justice: Trends and Patterns. 12(1):1-17.

Gaines, L. K., Kaune, M., and Miller, R. L. (2000). Criminal Justice in Action. Belmont, CA: Wadsworth-Thomson Learning.

Gaines, L. K., Kuane, M., and Miller, R. L. (2001). Criminal Justice in Action: The Core. Belmont, CA: Wadsworth Publishing Co.

Griffin, P. (2000). "National Overviews." State Juvenile Justice Profiles. Pittsburgh, PA: National Center for Juvenile Justice Online. Available online at http://ncjj.org./stateprofiles

Harms, P. (2002). Detention in Delinquency Cases, 1989-1998. Office of Juvenile Justice and Delinquency Prevention. U.S. Department of Justice. Washington, D.C.

Inciardi, J. A. (1999). Criminal Justice. (6th ed.). Fort Worth, TX: Harcourt Brace College Publishers.

Jacobson, J. (2002). "Trading Tenure for More Money." The Chronicle of Higher Education. August 28, Thursday.

Light, S. C. (1991). "Assaults on Prison Officers: Interactional Themes." Justice Quarterly, 8(2): 243 - 261.

Light, S. C. (1999). Understanding Criminal Justice. Belmont, CA: Wadsworth Publishing Co.

Messerschmidt, C. W. (1997). Crime as Structured Action: Gender, Race, Class, and Crime in the Making. Thousand Oaks, CA: Sage Publications.

National Center for Juvenile Justice (2002). "National Overviews." State Juvenile Justice Profiles. Pittsburgh, PA: NCJJ Online. Available online at http://ncjj.org./stateprofiles/.

Reddington, F., and Anderson, J. F. (1996). "Juveniles in Jails and the Legal Responsibilities: The More Things Change the More They Stay the Same." Journal of Juvenile Justice and Detention Services." 11(2):47-54.

Schmalleger, F. (2001). Criminal Justice Today: An Introductory Text for the 21st Century. (6th ed.).Upper Saddle River, New Jersey: Prentice Hall.

Senna, J. J., and Siegel, L. J. (2000). Essentials of Criminal Justice. (3rd ed.). Belmont, CAL West/Wadsworth Publishing Co.

Simonsen, C. E. (1991). Juvenile Justice in America. (3rd ed.). New York: Macmillan.

Smith, C. (1998). The American System of Criminal Justice. (8th ed.). Belmont, CA: Wadsworth Publishing Company.

Sontheimer, H., Goodstein, L., and Kovacevic, M. (1990). "Philadelphia Intensive Aftercare Probation Evaluation Project." Harrisburg: Pennsylvania Commission on Crime and Delinquency.

Staples, W. G. (1987). "Law and social control in juvenile justice dispositions." Journal of Research in Crime and Delinquency, 24:7-22.

Thomas, C. W., and Cage, R. (1977). "The effect of social characteristics on juvenile court dispositions." Sociological Quarterly, 18:237-252.

Thornberry, T. P. (1973). "Race, socioeconomic status and sentencing in the juvenile justice system." Journal of Criminal Law and Criminology 64:90-98.

Torbet, P. (1996). Juvenile Probation: The Workhorse of the Juvenile Justice System. Office of Juvenile Justice and Delinquency Prevention. Washington, D.C.: U.S. Department of Justice.

Torbet, P. and Szymanski, L. (1998). State Legislative Responses to Violent Juvenile Crime: 1996-97 Update. Office of Juvenile Justice and Delinquency Prevention. Washington, D.C.: U.S. Department of Justice.

Trojanowicz, R., Morash, M. and Schram, P. (2001). Juvenile Delinquency: Concepts and Control. (6th ed.). Englewood Cliffs, NJ: Prentice Hall, Inc.

Whitehead, J. T., and Lab, S. P. (1990). Juvenile Justice: An Introduction. Cincinnati, OH: Anderson Publishing.

PART TWO

Local, State, and Federal Positions

LOCAL POSITIONS

Aftercare Caseworker

Description:
Aftercare caseworkers provide case management for juveniles who are re-entering the community. They interview juveniles and their families to assess their social service needs and conduct support sessions. They update files on activities of youths and maintain contact with facility staff to monitor the child's re-entry process. Aftercare caseworkers work with other members of the local juvenile justice system, attend regular staff meetings, and may perform other related work as required.

Qualifications:
Applicants must have a valid driver's license and must pass a criminal background check. In addition, they must hold a bachelor's degree from an accredited college or university.

Education:
Applicants must have a bachelor's degree from an accredited college or university. The degree must be in criminal justice, social work, sociology, psychology, or a related field. Applicants should be aware that more education increases the likelihood of promotion and advancement.

Preferred/Required Skills:
1. Effective oral and written skills
2. Excellent interview techniques
3. Ability to observe and objectively evaluate various resident behaviors
4. Excellent evaluation and counseling skills
5. Ability to be decisive and use sound judgment
6. Ability to remain calm under stress and communicate well in a non-threatening manner
7. Bilingualism, especially in Spanish, is a plus

Training:
If hired, the applicant must successfully complete any required agency/state training.

Grade Level(s): Not applicable

What to Expect:
1. Employment history check
2. Criminal history check
3. Drug use history check
4. Personal history check
5. Applicant may encounter a waiting period
6. May involve drug testing

Salary Range:
This position pays a starting salary of approximately $25,000 per year.

Airport Police Officer

Description:
The duties of an Airport Police Officer require preserving the peace, enforcing laws and regulations, and providing protection for people and property within the airport authority's jurisdiction. Officers must be prepared to work in all types of weather, and may work evenings, weekends, holidays, and occasional overtime, depending on the assigned shift.

Qualifications:
Applicants must be U.S. citizens, be at least 21 years of age, and possess a valid driver's license. Current employment as a sworn officer is desired but not required. Applicants must pass a criminal background check, physical exam, written and psychological tests, drug testing, and must successfully complete all required training.

Education:
Applicants must have a minimum high school diploma or General Education Diploma for this position.

Preferred/Required Skills:
1. Effective oral and writing skills
2. Good interpersonal skills
3. Good problem-solving ability
4. Good judgment
5. Self-control

6.   Bilingualism is a plus, especially Spanish and Middle Eastern languages
7.   Sound mental and physical health

Training:
If hired, the applicant must successfully complete all required training, including police academy training and internal agency training.

Grade Level(s): Not applicable

What to Expect:
1.   Employment history check
2.   Criminal history check
3.   Drug use history check
4.   Personal history check
5.   Applicant may encounter a waiting period
6.   Drug testing

Salary Range:
The starting salary for this position is approximately $33,000 to $49,000, depending on qualifications and experience.

*Qualifications and salary will vary from state to state.

Assistant Community Corrections Officer

Description:
The responsibilities of an Assistant Community Corrections Officer include ensuring that adults released by the Courts under Community Supervision/Pre-trial Services receive supervision in court-directed rehabilitation and are in compliance with court directives. The position requires participation in the planning of programs, policies or objectives for one's own work group, or department, or other work groups and departments. Duties of the position include administering drug tests; conducting office visits with clients for counseling, screening; referral treatment and/or other related programs; initial interviewing of clients in the office; jail or other location under general supervision; supervision of electronic monitoring installation; and monitoring of ignition interlock

defendants; locating absconders or clients who fail to appear in court; and assistance with pre-sentence reports.

Qualifications:
Applicants must be certifiable as a Community Supervision Officer. Verbal and written bilingualism in Spanish is a plus for the position.

Education:
Applicants must possess a bachelor's degree from an accredited institution. Applicants should be aware that more education increases the likelihood of promotion and advancement.

Preferred/Required Skills:
1.   Effective oral and writing skills
2.   Good interpersonal skills
3.   Good problem solving ability
4.   Good judgment
5.   Self-control
6.   Bilingualism in Spanish
7.   Sound mental and physical health

Training:
Applicants must successfully complete all required agency/state training.

Grade Level(s): Not applicable

What to Expect:
1.   Employment history check
2.   Criminal history check
3.   Drug use history check
4.   Personal history check

Salary Range:
The salary for this position is approximately $24,000 per year.

*Qualifications and salary may vary from state to state.

Campus Police and Emergency Director (High School)

Description:
The responsibilities of the position include the supervision of staff members; coordination of emergency protocol and response plan; and the investigation of student violations. The Campus Police and Emergency Director is responsible for the day-to-day operations of the department, as well as overall campus safety. The Director will develop and implement a training program for campus resource officers, as well as an emergency response protocol, including walk-through scenarios. He or she will also be responsible for ensuring that safety training is provided for all employees.

Qualifications:
The position requires eight to ten years of law enforcement experience and law enforcement certification, or an equivalent combination of education and training. Preference is given to applicants with managerial experience and demonstrated leadership in an academic environment, and those with prior investigative, teaching, and training experience.

Education:
Applicants must have a bachelor's degree. Applicants should be aware that more education increases the likelihood of promotion and advancement.

Preferred/Required Skills:
1. Effective oral and writing skills
2. Good interpersonal skills
3. Good problem solving ability
4. Good judgment
5. Self-control
6. Leadership and management skills
7. Sound mental and physical health
8. Strong investigative background
9. Teaching and training

Training:
No specific agency/state training noted.

Grade Level(s): Not applicable

What to Expect:
1.   Employment history check
2.   Background check

Salary Range:
The salary for this position is commensurate with the applicant's education and experience.

Counselor, Community Supervision and Corrections

Description:
Counselors are responsible for the direct provision of counseling services. They conduct intake screening for potential residents, prepare psychosocial histories for residents on an assigned caseload, and perform individual and group counseling for residents and their families. Counselors develop individual treatment plans and aftercare plans for each resident on their caseload and work with outside agencies to provide appropriate referrals and services. Counselors also write assessment reports for the courts, including recommendations for treatment, and provide court testimony.

Qualifications:
Depending on the hiring agency, applicants will be required to be licensed as a professional counselor, social worker, marriage and family therapist, or other related credential. They may be required to work evenings or weekends and depending on the agency, may be required to use their own vehicle while on duty.

Education:
Applicants must have a bachelor's degree. Applicants should be aware that more education increases the likelihood of promotion and advancement.

Preferred/Required Skills:
1.   Effective oral and writing skills
2.   Knowledge of counseling theories and interventions
3.   Good interpersonal skills
4.   Ability to work with adult substance abuse clients
5.   Ability to administer group and individual counseling

6.   Bilingualism, especially Spanish

Training:
Applicants must successfully complete all required agency/state training.

Grade Level(s): Not applicable

What to Expect:
1.   Employment history check
2.   Criminal history check
3.   Drug use history check
4.   Personal history check
5.   Applicant may encounter a waiting period
6.   May involve drug testing

Salary Range:
The salary for this position is approximately $28,000 per year.

*Salary and qualifications may vary by agency.

Court Operations Clerk (Bond forfeiture)

Description:
Court clerks perform data entry of case information; issue and mail citations and notices; answer questions from the public; calculate and collect fees; produce legal documents according to judicial orders; prepare the court docket; notify, by mail, lawsuit parties of court hearings; attend court hearings; research criminal cases, appeals, and dismissal information; and perform other tasks related to position.

Qualifications:
Applicants must pass a typing test, have a valid driver's license, valid insurance, and a personal vehicle. The position requires knowledge of general office procedures; knowledge of court procedures and legal terminology; the ability to understand criminal, civil, and probate codes, as well as bond forfeiture; and the ability to accurately enter data.

Education:
Applicants must have a minimum high school diploma or General Education Diploma for this position.

Preferred/Required Skills:
1.   Clerical skills
2.   Computer skills
3.   Organizational skills
4.   Interpersonal skills

Training:
Applicants must successfully complete all required training.

Grade Level(s): Not applicable

What to Expect:
1.   Employment history check
2.   Interview

Salary Range:
The salary for this position is approximately $18,348 per year.

*The example is for Bexar County, Texas. Salary and qualifications may vary by state and agency.

Court Reporter

Description:
Court reporters transcribe court proceedings and legal depositions. They may be independent contractors or salaried employees. Independent contractors usually charge fees based on the number of pages of transcription, how soon the completed transcription is required, and travel expenses.

Qualifications:
The qualifications for this position include successful completion of course work and certification, if mandated by the state.

Education:
The amount of education required to become a court reporter usually entails two years of courses on court reporting.

Preferred/Required Skills:
1. Language skills
2. Excellent manual dexterity
3. Organizational skills
4. Ability to work independently

Training:
No specific agency/state training noted.

Grade Level(s): Not applicable

What to Expect:
1. Interview

Salary Range:
The salary range for court reporters is approximately $45,000 to $75,000 per year.

Criminalist

Description:
Criminalists collect, process, and maintain evidence from crime scenes and fatal accidents, and log and secure evidence and/or property into the property room. They photograph crime scenes, and develop and print mug photographs of suspects from jail. They identify and process latent fingerprints and fingerprint citizens and children for various purposes. Criminalists perform field tests on drugs when necessary; testify in court; and may enforce local, state, and federal laws if the position is filled by a law enforcement officer.

Qualifications:
The position requires an advanced level of training in latent prints and crime scene investigation, plus at least two years experience. It also requires a valid driver's license. Depending on the agency, being a sworn law enforcement officer is desirable.

Education:
The position requires a minimum high school diploma or General Education Diploma or an associate's degree, depending on the agency. Some agencies require a specified number of forensics-related college courses.

Preferred/Required Skills:
1. Self-motivation
2. Good interpersonal skills
3. Technically accurate judgment
4. Ability to work effectively in a team environment
5. Ability to perform multiple tasks simultaneously
6. Good organizational and communication skills
7. Reliability and positive attitude

Training:
Applicants must successfully complete all required agency/state training.

Grade Level(s): Not applicable

What to Expect:
1. Employment history check
2. Criminal history check
3. Drug use history check
4. Personal history check
5. Applicant may encounter a waiting period

Salary Range:
The salary for this position is based on experience and qualifications.

Deputy Sheriff

Description:
The duties and responsibilities of this position include patrol, drug interdiction, prisoner transports, security services, and civil process tasks.

Qualifications:
Applicants must be at least 21 years of age with a high school diploma, no felony convictions, and be a U.S. citizen or permanent resident alien who

has applied for citizenship. Applicants must pass an extensive background investigation, written test, psychological evaluation, medical examination, polygraph testing, physical agility test, and successfully complete all required training.

Education:
The position requires a minimum high school diploma or General Education Diploma. Applicants should be aware that more education increases the likelihood of promotion and advancement.

Preferred/Required Skills:
1.   Effective oral and writing skills
2.   Good interpersonal skills
3.   Good problem solving ability
4.   Good judgment
5.   Self-control
6.   Bilingualism is a plus, especially in Spanish and Middle Eastern languages
7.   Sound mental and physical health

Training:
If hired, applicants must complete six months of training.

Grade Level(s): Not applicable

What to Expect:
1.   Employment history check
2.   Criminal history check
3.   Drug use history check
4.   Personal history check
5.   Applicant may encounter a waiting period
6.   May involve drug testing
7.   Polygraph testing

Salary Range:
The salary for this position is $41,459 to $63,736 per year.

* Salary will vary by state and agency. The example is for San Diego County, California.

Detention Officer (Juvenile)

Description:
Detention Officers assist the detention control room person as well as the detention floor staff in daily operations of the detention facility. Detention officers maintain a safe, secure detention atmosphere; attend to youth's emotional and physical needs; monitor group dynamics to prevent fights and escapes; monitor detainees in their rooms; supervise detainees; screen visitors; conduct room searches; search detainees, as required; maintain rosters and logbooks; assist in the completion of referral paperwork; aid in court security; and perform other duties as assigned.

Qualifications:
Applicants must have a valid driver's license, a telephone number at which they can be reached, and access to a vehicle that can be used while on duty. Preference is given to applicants who have college credits or work experience in a related field.

Education:
The position requires a minimum high school diploma or General Education Diploma. Applicants should be aware that more education increases the likelihood of promotion and advancement.

Preferred/Required Skills:
1.   Ability to work effectively with adolescents
2.   Understanding of adolescent behavioral patterns
3.   Good judgment
4.   Friendly and cheerful disposition
5.   Ability to work well with others
6.   Dedication and flexibility

Training:
Applicants must successfully complete all required agency/state training.

Grade Level(s): Not applicable

What to Expect:
1.   Employment history check
2.   Criminal history check
3.   Drug use history check

4. Personal history check
5. Applicant may encounter a waiting period
6. May involve drug testing

Salary Range:
The salary for this position is $19,786 per year.

*This example is for Montgomery County, Texas. Salary and qualifications may vary by state.

Detention Officer I, Probation (Juvenile)

Description:
Juvenile detention officers supervise daily activities and behavior of juveniles in a detention center. They monitor living conditions, visitation with families, and youth interaction; prepare behavior and incident reports on detainees; transport juveniles; conduct body searches; and perform related duties as required.

Qualifications:
Applicants must be at least 21 years of age, have a valid driver's license, be state certified as a Juvenile Detention Officer, and be certified in first aid and physical restraint techniques within sixty days of employment. Applicants must have at least an associate's degree from an accredited college or university and one year of experience, or a combination of education and experience that is acceptable. Applicants must pass a background check, pre-employment physical exam, and psychological assessment.

Education:
The position requires a minimum high school diploma or associate's degree. Applicants should be aware that more education increases the likelihood of promotion and advancement.

Preferred/Required Skills:
1. Interpersonal skills
2. Knowledge of juvenile detention practices and procedures

Training:
Applicants must successfully complete all required agency/state training.

Grade Level(s): Not applicable

What to Expect:
1. Employment history check
2. Background investigation
3. Psychological exam
4. Physical exam

Salary Range:
The salary range for this position is $21,816 per year.

*This example is for Bexar County, Texas. Salary and qualifications may vary by state.

Emergency Communications Director (911)

Description:
The responsibilities of the Emergency Communications Director include planning, developing, organizing and directing all aspects of the center; ensuring compliance with applicable federal and state regulations; budget preparation and management; administering all staffing and personnel functions; providing information and reports to county, state, and federal officials; and acting as the liaison with all involved jurisdictions, as well as the public.

Qualifications:
The position requires approximately five years of progressively responsible experience in a senior management or administrative capacity, or an equivalent combination of education and experience. A law enforcement background with 911 communications experience is desirable.

Education:
A bachelor's degree with major course work in criminal justice, business management, public administration, communications or a related area is required.

Preferred/Required Skills:
1. Excellent management skills
2. Good oral and written communication skills

Training:
No specific agency/state training noted.

Grade Level(s): Not applicable

What to Expect:
1. Employment history check
2. Criminal history check
3. Drug use history check
4. Personal history check
5. Applicant may encounter a waiting period
6. May involve drug testing

Salary Range:
The salary range for this position is $51,000 to $69,000 per year.

*Qualifications and salary will vary by state and agency.

Emergency Dispatcher (Public Safety Dispatcher or Communications Dispatcher)

Description:
The duties of the position include: receiving emergency and non-emergency calls; eliciting pertinent information from callers; recording information; dispatching police, fire and medical units on a two-way radio system; operating the dispatch console; maintaining department records; operating various criminal justice computer systems which require a high level of confidentiality; performing a variety of office assignments; providing information; and referring calls to appropriate personnel.

Qualifications:
The position requires the possession of or ability to obtain a POST (Peace Officer Standards and Training) dispatcher certification. A combination of education and experience likely to provide the required knowledge and abilities is required if the applicant does not already have POST

certification. Bilingualism is a plus for this position.

Education:
Applicants must have a minimum high school diploma or General Education Diploma for this position.

Preferred/Required Skills:
1.   Effective oral and writing skills
2.   Good interpersonal skills
3.   Ability to calm people who are under stress
4.   Good judgment
5.   Self-control
6.   Bilingualism

Training:
Applicants must successfully complete all required agency/state training.

Grade Level(s): Not applicable

What to Expect:
1.   Employment history check
2.   Criminal history check
3.   Drug use history check
4.   Personal history check
5.   Applicant may encounter a waiting period
6.   May involve drug testing
7.   Psychological and medical evaluation
8.   Probation period

Salary Range:
The salary range for this position is approximately $24,000 to $48,000 per year, depending on agency, experience, and qualifications.

Fraud Analyst, Manager

Description:
Fraud analysts develop, modify and determine the effectiveness of fraud detection rules and establish metrics to measure fraud standards. The position involves the identification of tool kits to support fraud

management and focuses on vulnerabilities and prioritization of developmental infrastructure.

Qualifications:
The position requires extensive experience in fraud management; a demonstrated ability to perform operational analyses pertaining to fraud; database programming skills; statistical analysis and technologies for fraud modeling; and the ability to execute strategic planning to optimize management of fraud policy.

Education:
A specific amount of education is not listed for this position.

Preferred/Required Skills:
1.   Excellent analytical skills
2.   Extensive knowledge of fraud management
3.   Good oral and written communication skills

Training:
No specific agency/state training noted.

Grade Level(s): Not applicable

What to Expect:
1.   Employment history check
2.   Interview

Salary Range:
The salary range for this position is $75,000 to $110,000 per year.

Intake Interviewer (Juvenile)

Description:
Intake Interviewers are responsible for interviewing adolescents and parents; performing structured observations; data management; assisting in the preparation of reports; and facilitating relations with program and corrections staff. Travel to neighborhoods using public transportation is required, in addition to site visits to incarcerated youth.

Qualifications:
Applicants must have a bachelor's degree. Preference is given to candidates with experience working with adolescents or incarcerated populations, experience with social science field research, and cross-cultural experience. It is helpful, in many cases, to be fluent in Spanish.

Education:
A bachelor's degree is required for this position. Applicants should be aware that more education increases the likelihood of promotion and advancement.

Preferred/Required Skills:
1.   Excellent interpersonal relations skills
2.   Research skills
3.   Strong writing skills
4.   Good organizational skills

Training:
No specific agency/state training noted.

Grade Level(s): Not applicable

What to Expect:
1.   Employment history check
2.   Interview

Salary Range:
The salary range is commensurate with the qualifications and experience of the applicant.

*This example is for the Vera Institute of Justice in New York. Salary and qualifications may vary by state and agency.

Intake Specialist (Juvenile)

Description:
Intake Specialists are responsible for the placement of youth referred to the agency. They receive and review youth referral and intake information from care management staff; place youth in agency foster homes and

alternative placements; maintain a close working relationship with public and private agencies involved in providing services and support to children and families; coordinate transportation of youth; complete documentation and forward reports; present information to management and public groups; and perform other duties related to the position.

Qualifications:
A bachelor's degree in a social service field is required. Experience in juvenile intake services is preferred. The position requires statistical and computational skills, good analytical skills, and the ability to interpret common scientific and technical journals, financial reports, and legal documents.

Education:
A bachelor's degree is required for this position. Applicants should be aware that more education increases the likelihood of promotion and advancement.

Preferred/Required Skills:
1.   Effective oral and writing skills
2.   Good interpersonal skills
3.   Computer skills
4.   Analytical and presentation skills

Training:
No specific agency/state training noted.

Grade Level(s): Not applicable

What to Expect:
1.   Employment history check
2.   Interview

Salary Range:
The salary range for this position is commensurate with qualifications and experience.

*This example is for The Farm, Inc. in New York. Salary and qualifications may vary by agency and state.

Jailor, County Sheriff's Office

Description:
Jailers supervise, secure, control and care for inmates in the detention center. They observe conduct and behavior of inmates to prevent disturbances and escapes; inspect all areas of assigned work areas; maintain direct contact with inmates in order to provide prompt resolution of problems; supervise and maintain housekeeping procedures; prepare detailed reports in regard to incidents within the facility; employ force to maintain discipline and order when necessary; and perform other duties as directed.

Qualifications:
Applicants must be at least 19 years of age, must not have a felony conviction or be on probation, and must pass a criminal background investigation. They must pass a written entrance exam, psychological testing, physical agility test, and must pass all requirements for state certification in order to qualify for Jailor's Certification.

Education:
A minimum high school diploma or General Education Diploma is required for this position.

Preferred/Required Skills:
1.   Good interpersonal skills
2.   Good judgment
3.   Good self-control

Training:
All required agency/state training must be successfully completed.

Grade Level(s): Not applicable

What to Expect:
1.   Employment history check
2.   Background investigation
3.   Written test
4.   Psychological testing
5.   Physical test
6.   Interview

Salary Range:
The minimum salary for this position is $24,792 per year.

*This example is for Bexar County, Texas. Salary and qualifications may vary by state and agency.

Outreach Worker II (Juvenile)

Description:
Outreach workers provide in-depth counseling to detainees on substance abuse, crisis intervention, mental health, and conflict resolution. They conduct group and individual counseling sessions; wake up and bedtime procedures; unit housekeeping; perform security checks; supervise detainees; and prepare reports.

Qualifications:
Applicants must pass a background check. Applicants must also have four years of experience working with and counseling adolescents. Preference will be given to those with a bachelor's degree in psychology, social work, sociology, or criminal justice.

Education:
The position requires a minimum high school diploma or associate's degree. Applicants should be aware that more education increases the likelihood of promotion and advancement.

Preferred/Required Skills:
1.   Excellent counseling skills
2.   Excellent interpersonal skills
3.   Effective writing skills
4.   Good judgment and responsible attitude

Training:
No specific agency/state training noted.

Grade Level(s): S17

What to Expect:
1.   Employment history check

2.   Background check
3.   Interview

Salary Range: The salary range for this position is $28,000 to $38,000.

*This example is for Fairfax County, Virginia. Salary and qualifications may vary by state.

Police Commander

Description:
The Commander directs and manages a major division of the Police Department. This is a senior management position which reports directly to the Chief of Police.

Qualifications:
The minimum qualification for this position is seven years of municipal police experience with four years as a sergeant or above. Candidates must possess an Advanced and Supervisory POST (Peace Officer Standards and Training) Certificate.

Education:
A bachelor's degree is required for this position. Applicants should be aware that more education may increase the likelihood of promotion and advancement.

Preferred/Required Skills:
1.   Management skills
2.   Effective oral and writing skills
3.   Good problem solving ability

Training:
No specific agency/state training noted.

Grade Level(s): Not applicable

What to Expect:
1.   Employment history check
2.   Criminal history check

3.   Drug use history check
4.   Personal history check
5.   Applicant may encounter a waiting period
6.   May involve drug testing

Salary Range:
The salary range for this position depends on the agency and area. Urban areas may pay more than $60,000 per year.

Police Communications Operator (Dispatcher)

Description:
Police Communications Operators perform a full range of duties which include: (1) receiving emergency and non-emergency calls; (2) eliciting pertinent information from callers; (3) recording information; (4) dispatching police, fire, and medical units; and (5) maintaining records and other assignments.

Qualifications:
A high school diploma and one year of telephone/switchboard experience is required for this position. Appropriate college course work or vocational or technical training may substitute at an equivalent rate for required experience. Proficiency in typing and State Certification on NCIC/FCIC computer system (department will train) is required. The ability to communicate effectively by phone and police radio, and the ability to handle several functions simultaneously while under a high degree of stress is critical for this position.

Education:
A minimum high school diploma or General Education Diploma is required for this position. More education may increase the likelihood of promotion and advancement.

Preferred/Required Skills:
1.   Ability to do multiple tasks under stress
2.   Good interpersonal skills
3.   Good problem solving ability
4.   Good judgment
5.   Self-control

6.   Effective oral and writing skills
7.   Bilingualism, especially Spanish, is a plus
8.   Sound mental and physical health

Training:
The amount of training required depends on the experience of the applicant.

Grade Level(s): Not applicable

What to Expect:
1.   Employment history check
2.   Criminal history check
3.   Drug use history check
4.   Personal history check
5.   Applicant may encounter a waiting period
6.   May involve drug testing

Salary Range:
The salary range for this position varies from about $22,000 to $52,000 per year. Positions at some agencies start as high as $40,000 per year.

*Salary and qualifications vary by agency and area.

Police Communications Operator, Senior

Description:
The Senior Police Communications Operator supervises police communications operators and the operation of the Police Department's Communications Dispatch Center.

Qualifications:
The position requires three years of telephone/switchboard experience. Proficiency in typing and State Certification in the FCIC/NCIC computer system (certification can be obtained after employment) is required. Preference is given to applicants with supervisory experience.

Education:
A minimum high school diploma or associate's degree is required for this

position. More education may increase the likelihood of promotion and advancement.

Preferred/Required Skills:
1. Supervisory skills
2. Good interpersonal skills
3. Ability to perform multiple tasks under stressful conditions
4. Good judgment
5. Effective oral and written communication skills
6. Bilingualism, especially in Spanish, is a plus
7. Sound mental and physical health

Training:
No specific agency/state training noted.

Grade Level(s): Not applicable

What to Expect:
1. Employment history check
2. Criminal history check
3. Drug use history check
4. Personal history check
5. Applicant may encounter a waiting period
6. May involve drug testing

Salary Range:
The salary for this position is dependent upon the experience and qualifications of the candidate.

*Salary and qualifications may vary by agency.

Police Officer

Description:
Police officers provide service to the communities they serve by maintaining order and enforcing the laws. The bulk of police work is service-oriented (answering calls for information, responding to emergencies, calming disputing parties, traffic control, accident investigation). The police also combat crime by responding to calls,

making arrests, investigating crimes, performing proactive crime fighting tasks, and patrolling. Police agencies have a variety of patrol methods, including foot patrol, bicycle patrol, automobile patrol, horse patrol, lake or harbor patrol, and air patrol, depending upon the needs of the community. Larger agencies have specialized units, such as vice, juvenile, and investigation.

Qualifications:
Qualifications for police officers vary by agency and state. Some jurisdictions require a bachelor's degree or associate degree, while others require a high school diploma or the equivalent. Most agencies require applicants to be at least 21 years of age, and many limit applicants to those 35 years old or younger. Applicants must not have been convicted of a felony, and there are often limitations on misdemeanor convictions. Applicants must pass all pre-screening requirements, which usually include psychological tests, extensive background investigation; written test; physical examination; and polygraph testing. In addition, recruits must successfully complete police academy training, and may be required to obtain state certification. New officers are generally on probation for a specified period of time.

Education:
Depending on the state and agency, police officers are required to have a minimum high school diploma. Applicants should be aware that more education increases the likelihood of promotion and advancement.

Preferred/Required Skills:
1.   Excellent interpersonal skills
2.   Ability to perform duties with minimal supervision
3.   Ability to work effectively as part of a team
4.   Oral and written skills

Training:
The position requires successful completion of the police academy and in-service training throughout the career. Some jurisdictions require state certification.

Grade Level(s):
Police agencies are quasi-military organizations. Officers progress from recruit to line officer, sergeant, lieutenant, captain, division commander,

and up to the chief of police.

What to Expect:
1. Extensive background investigation
2. Psychological and physical exams
3. Written exams
4. Polygraph testing
5. Drug testing

Salary Range:
Police officers may be paid anywhere from $20,000 to $65,000 per year, depending on the area and agency. Police salaries vary widely, depending on whether they are in urban or rural areas, area cost of living, and seniority of the officer. Some small towns may pay less, and urban areas with a high cost of living may pay senior officers more. Examples of police salaries include:

Bartlesville, OK: $23,000; Gulfport, MS: $23,628 starting salary; Tampa, FL: $32,211-$45,337; Lakewood, CO: $38,505 - $57,331; San Jose, CA: $51,688 starting salary; Decatur, IL: $36,933 - $54,339; Richmond, VA: $30,426 - $67,516; Bryan, TX: $31,500 - $48,300.

Police Officer/Pilot

Description:
Police Officer/Pilots fly aircraft as part of their law enforcement duties.

Qualifications:
Applicants must be certified law enforcement officers, may be required to have a pilot's license, and must successfully complete flight training.

Education:
The position requires a minimum high school diploma or General Education Diploma. Applicants should be aware that more education increases the likelihood of promotion and advancement.

Preferred/Required Skills:
1. Law enforcement skills
2. Flying skills

3.   Good judgment
4.   Sound mental and physical health

Training:
If hired, the applicant must successfully complete training, first as an observer, then as a pilot.

Grade Level(s): No specific agency/state training noted.

What to Expect:
1.   Employment history check
2.   Criminal history check
3.   Drug use history check
4.   Personal history check
5.   Applicant may encounter a waiting period
6.   May involve drug testing

Salary Range:
The salary range for this position is $25,000 to $80,000 per year, depending on the experience and qualifications of the candidate.

*Salary and qualifications may vary by agency.

Probation and Parole Officer (Trainee)

Description:
Probation and parole officers perform community supervision of adult offenders released on probation or parole to ensure that clients adhere to the rules and regulations of probation and/or parole. They perform pre-sentence and pre-parole investigations; prepare summaries and reports; attend and present information at court hearings; meet with probationers and parolees; and participate in arrests and transportation of clients.

Qualifications:
Applicants must have a bachelor's degree, pass oral interviews, pass written tests, pass a background investigation, and successfully complete a writing sample.

Education:
A bachelor's degree is required for this position. More education increases the likelihood of promotion and advancement.

Preferred/Required Skills:
1. Interpersonal skills
2. Writing skills
3. Investigative skills

Training:
Candidates must successfully complete all required agency/state training.

Grade Level(s): Not applicable

What to Expect:
1. Employment history check
2. Interview
3. Background investigation
4. Written test

Salary Range:
This position pays an approximate starting salary of $25,000.

*Salary and qualifications may vary by state and agency.

Probation Officer, Field Services (Juvenile)

Description:
Under the supervision of the Supervisor of Field Services, Probation Officers – Field Services perform moderately complex service work in providing probationary supervision and counseling to juveniles directed by the court. They supervise probationers in their homes, schools, and places of employment. They monitor the supervision and treatment provided by other juvenile service agencies; attend all court hearings related to assigned cases; develop, review, and implement treatment plans; prepare caseload reports; and transport probationers to appointments and court appearances.

Qualifications:
Applicants must have a bachelor's degree and one year of experience in full- time casework or related social service, or one year of graduate study in criminology, social work, or a related approved field. They must have a valid driver's license, use of a vehicle to be used on duty, and a telephone number where they can be reached.

Education:
The position requires a bachelor's degree from an accredited college or university. Applicants should be aware that more education increases the likelihood of promotion and advancement.

Preferred/Required Skills:
1.   Commitment to develop people to their full potential
2.   Working knowledge of the principles and techniques of social case work
3.   Working knowledge of the laws and procedures applicable to preparation of case documents
4.   Good interpersonal skills

Training:
No specific agency/state training noted.

Grade Level(s): Not applicable

What to Expect:
1.   Employment history check
2.   Background check
3.   Interview
4.   May involve drug testing

Salary Range:
The starting salary for this position is $26,000 per year.

*This example is for Montgomery County, Texas. Salary and qualifications vary by state.

Referral Counselor (Juvenile)

Description:
This position involves directing and assisting youth and their families by means of assessment, counseling and/or referral. Employees confer with law enforcement personnel, school officials, courts, and other human services agencies on youth-oriented problems. Supervision may be exercised over clerical or auxiliary staff or volunteer workers.

Qualifications:
Applicants are tested over their knowledge, skills, and/or abilities in such areas as adolescent counseling, adolescent development, interviewing, and preparing written material. A bachelor's degree from an accredited college or university, plus one year of professional counseling experience or an acceptable combination of education and experience is required. Applicants may be required to pass a pre-employment drug test.

Education:
A bachelor's degree is required for this position. Applicants should be aware that more education increases the likelihood of promotion and advancement.

Preferred/Required Skills:
1.   Excellent counseling and interviewing skills.
2.   Effective writing skills.
3.   Excellent interpersonal skills.
4.   Ability to work independently

Training:
No specific agency/state training noted.

Grade Level(s): Not applicable

What to Expect:
1.   Employment history check
2.   Criminal history check
3.   May require drug testing
4.   Interview

Salary Range:
The salary range for this position is $31,000 to $40,000 per year.

*This example is for Monroe County, New York. The salary and qualifications may vary by state.

Residential Treatment Officer I, Probation (Juvenile)

Description:
Residential Treatment Officers supervise daily activities and behavior of juveniles in a correctional center. They monitor living conditions; conduct therapeutic group meetings with juveniles and collaborate with treatment staff; monitor youth interaction and maintain authority and youth compliance with established procedures; transport juveniles; monitor visitation; conduct body searches; and perform related duties as required.

Qualifications:
Applicants must be at least 21 years of age, have a valid driver's license, be state certified as a Juvenile Detention Officer. Applicants must have at least an associate's degree from an accredited college or university and one year of experience, or a combination of education and experience. Applicants must pass a background check, pre-employment physical exam, and psychological assessment.

Education:
This position requires a minimum associate's degree. Applicants should be aware that more education increases the likelihood of promotion and advancement.

Preferred/Required Skills:
1. Good interpersonal skills
2. Effective oral and written communication skills
3. Knowledge of juvenile probation practices and techniques

Training:
Candidates must complete all required training, including certification in first aid and physical restraint techniques within the first 60 days of employment.

Grade Level(s): Not applicable

What to Expect
1.   Employment history check
2.   Background investigation
3.   Psychological exam
4.   Physical exam

Salary Range:
The salary for this position is $21,816 per year.

*This example is for Bexar County, Texas. Salary and qualifications may vary by state.

School Resource Officer

Description:
School Resource Officers patrol school campuses; interact with students and faculty; handle truancy problems; educate students in the areas of alcohol and drug abuse; handle daily requests from principals and staff; participate in daily school functions; provide daily crisis intervention; and hold group sessions and meetings.

Qualifications:
School Resource Officers are sworn police officers and may be required to be state certified.

Education:
The position requires a high school diploma or General Education Diploma. More education may increase the likelihood of promotion and advancement.

Preferred/Required Skills:
1.   Law enforcement skills
2.   Good interpersonal skills
3.   Good problem solving ability
4.   Good judgment
5.   Self-control
6.   Bilingualism, especially in Spanish

7.   Sound mental and physical health
8.   Oral and written communication skills

Training:
If hired, the candidate must successfully complete all required training.

Grade Level(s): Not applicable

What to Expect:
1.   Employment history check
2.   Criminal history check
3.   Drug use history check
4.   Personal history check
5.   Applicant may encounter a waiting period
6.   May involve drug testing

Salary Range:
The starting salary for this position is $21,000, depending on the agency and area.

*Salary and qualifications may vary by agency.

School Safety and Crime Prevention Program Manager

Description:
The responsibilities and duties of this position include initiating and maintaining contact with middle and high school officials for their program implementation; scheduling, coordinating, and implementing training on program for staff, teachers, administrators and law enforcement personnel in each middle school and high school in the district; scheduling the delivery of a printed material and videotapes to each participating school; being the primary speaker for speaking engagements; drafting all grant required program and budget reports for submission to grant funding agency; preparing media releases and maintaining statistics as provided by the Police Detail regarding the program; and working under the supervision of the Administrative Director.

Qualifications:
The position requires appropriate skills and experience.

Education:
A minimum high school diploma or General Education Diploma is required for this position. More education may increase the likelihood of promotion and advancement.

Preferred/Required Skills:
1. Effective oral and writing skills
2. Good interpersonal skills
3. Good problem-solving skills
4. Ability to make effective public presentations
5. Ability to work as a team and independently
6. Good organizational skills

Training:
If hired, candidates must successfully complete all required agency/state training.

Grade Level(s): Not applicable

What to Expect:
1. Employment history check
2. Criminal history check
3. Drug use history check
4. Personal history check
5. Applicant may encounter a waiting period
6. May involve drug testing

Salary Range:
The starting alary for this position is $21,000 per year.

*Salary and qualifications may vary by agency.

School Safety Field Trainers

Description:
School Safety Field Trainers train school safety agents in a classroom setting as to how positive reinforcement leads to behavior change, how they can become skilled observers of positive behavior, and how they can use reinforcement techniques to effectively shape and support positive

student behavior. Trainers will then walk alongside safety agents in their schools throughout the day, giving them daily guidance on their positive reinforcement techniques. The position may require working evening hours when needed.

Qualifications:
A bachelor's degree is required for this position. A graduate degree in the social sciences is viewed favorably. Applicants must have three years of experience working with urban youth. Applicants must send a cover letter and resume.

Education:
The position requires at least a bachelor's degree. Applicants should be aware that more education increases the likelihood of promotion and advancement.

Preferred/Required Skills:
1.   Excellent presentation and people skills
2.   Classroom skills
3.   Computerized database skills

Training:
No specific agency/state training noted.

Grade Level(s): Not applicable

What to Expect:
1.   Interview

Salary Range:
The starting salary for this position is $37,000 per year, depending on education level.

*This example is for the Vera Institute of Justice in New York.

Security Police Officer (Entry Level)

Description:
This position is for a non-certified Security Police Officer at a large mall. Responsibilities include assisting sworn officers in their general law enforcement duties; taking non-arrest reports; patrolling in scout cars and on foot; enforcing the center's rules and regulations; and responding to emergencies. This position has the possibility of advancement to a sworn position.

Qualifications:
The position requires a minimum of a high school diploma or General Education Diploma, approved driving record, no criminal history, and achieving a passing score on the written test.

Education:
A minimum high school diploma or General Education Diploma is required. More education increases the likelihood of promotion and advancement.

Preferred/Required Skills:
1. Effective oral and writing skills
2. Good interpersonal skills
3. Good problem solving ability
4. Good judgment
5. Self-control
6. Bilingualism, especially in Spanish
7. Sound mental and physical health

Training:
Depends on experience

Grade Level(s): Not applicable

What to Expect:
1. Employment history check
2. Background check
3. Written exam

Salary Range:
The salary for this position can vary from minimum wage up to about $20,000 per year.

STATE POSITIONS

Assistant Court Analyst

Description:
Assistant Court Analysts provide professional level assistance to Court Analysts and higher level personnel in the Analyst Series in projects involving personnel, administration, budget development and court finance administration, resource allocation, and policy formation.

Qualifications:
The position requires one year as a Junior Court Analyst, or a bachelor's degree from an accredited college or university, or an equivalent combination of experience and education.

Education:
The position requires a bachelor's degree, depending on the experience of the applicant. Applicants should be aware that more education increases the likelihood of promotion and advancement.

Preferred/Required Skills:
1. Record keeping skills
2. Statistical skills
3. Payroll skills
4. Interpersonal skills

Training:
No specific agency/state training noted.

Grade Level(s): beginning at JG-16

What to Expect:
1. Employment history check
2. Interview

Salary Range:
The starting salary for this position is $35,367 plus $1,200 location pay per year.

*This example is for New York state. Salary and qualifications may vary by state and agency.

Chief Clerk IV JG-32

Description:
Chief Clerks are the highest ranking non-judicial employees in Supreme and County, City, Family and Surrogate Courts. Chief Clerks are responsible to judges, regional court administrators, and the Office of Court Administration for managing all aspects of court operation and non-judicial case processing activities. They supervise subordinate personnel; allocate court resources; prepare annual budget requests; make employee selection decisions; and are responsible for the receipt, accounting and disbursement of fines, bail fees, and other public or custodial fines.

Qualifications:
The position requires a bachelor's degree from an accredited college or university and five years of work experience involving managerial responsibilities, or an equivalent combination of education and experience.

Education:
A bachelor's degree is required for this position. Applicants should be aware that more education increases the likelihood of promotion and advancement.

Preferred/Required Skills:
1.   Excellent managerial skills
2.   Good knowledge of court system
3.   Interpersonal skills

Training:
No specific agency/state training noted.

Grade Level(s): JG-32

What to Expect:
1. Employment history check
2. Interview

Salary Range:
The starting salary for this position is $84,568 plus $1,200 location pay per year.

*This example is for New York state. Salary and qualifications may vary by state and agency.

Correctional Officer

Description:
A correctional officer is an entry level State civil service peace officer. Correctional Officers are responsible for protecting the public, staff, and inmates in a multitude of areas inside and outside prison walls.

Qualifications:
Applicants must have no felony convictions; be a U.S. citizen or permanent resident alien who is eligible for and has applied for U.S. citizenship prior to the completion of the background investigation; have a high school diploma, General Education Diploma or higher level degree; and have a history of law-abiding behavior.

Education:
The position requires a minimum high school diploma or General Education Diploma. More education may increase the likelihood of promotion and advancement.

Preferred/Required Skills:
1. Good interpersonal skills
2. Effective oral and written communication skills
3. Good problem solving ability
4. Good judgment
5. Self-control
6. Bilingualism is a plus, especially in Spanish
7. Sound mental and physical health

Training:
Correction officers must complete a sixteen-week, formal, comprehensive training program, passing all tests.

Grade Level(s): Not applicable

What to Expect:
1. Employment history check
2. Criminal history check
3. Drug use history check
4. Personal history check
5. Applicant may encounter a waiting period
6. May involve drug testing
7. Medical examination

Salary Range:
The salary range for this position is $33,708 to $54,876 per year.

*This example is for California. Salary and qualifications may vary by state.

Correctional Officer (Juvenile)

Description:
Youth Correctional Officers work in institutions, camps, drug treatment centers or special community programs. Their duties include security, supervision and custody of an assigned group of youth offenders in their daily living and activity programs. This is a peace officer classification, and in order to become a peace officer, applicants must meet specific physical, medical, personal, and special characteristic requirements.

Qualifications:
Applicants must be at least 21 years of age and either a U.S. citizen or a permanent resident alien who is eligible for and has applied for citizenship. Applicants must not be restricted from carrying a firearm as part of employment or have been convicted of a felony.

Education:
The position requires a minimum high school diploma or General

Education Diploma. Applicants should be aware that more education increases the likelihood of promotion and advancement.

Preferred/Required Skills and desirable qualities:
1.   Leadership
2.   Emotional maturity
3.   Empathy and understanding of juvenile problems
4.   Acceptance of racial, ethnic, and cultural differences
5.   Keenness of observation
6.   Professional attitude and appearance
7.   Physical, emotional, and mental soundness
8.   Effective writing skills

Training:
Selected candidates must successfully complete the training academy.

Grade Level(s): Peace Officer Classification

What to expect:
1.   Written test
2.   Eligibility test
3.   Hiring interview
4.   Vision and physical ability tests
5.   Background investigation
6.   Psychological evaluation
7.   Medical evaluation

Salary Range:
The salary range for this position is $25,000 to $48,000 per year.

*This example is for California. Salary and qualifications may vary by state.

Corrections Warden

Description:
Under administrative direction of the Regional Administrator of the Institutions Division, a warden is in charge of a state correctional institution for adults. The warden plans; organizes; directs and coordinates

all correctional, business management, work-training incentive programs; educational, medical and allied services; and related programs within a correctional institution. A warden formulates and executes a progressive program for the care, treatment, training, discipline, custody, and employment of inmates.

Qualifications:
Wardens are sworn peace officers and are subject to meeting all requirements of a peace officer. They must be a U.S. citizen, free from felony convictions, and at least 21 years of age. They must pass a background investigation, medical examination, and have successfully completed training as a peace officer.

Education:
The position requires a minimum bachelor's degree.

Preferred/Required Skills:
1. Excellent management skills
2. Good interpersonal skills
3. Good problem-solving ability
4. Good oral and written communication skills

Training:
Wardens must have successfully completed peace officer training.

Grade Level(s): Not applicable

What to Expect:
1. Employment history check
2. Criminal history check
3. Drug use history check
4. Personal history check
5. May involve drug testing
6. Medical examination

Salary Range:
The salary range for this position is $75,640 to $103,416 per year.

*This example is for California: salary and qualifications may vary by state.

Criminal Intelligence Analyst: Department of Public Safety

Description:
Criminal Intelligence Analysts perform detailed research and analysis of criminal intelligence information. Their work involves analyzing data, writing reports, and developing links between criminals and crime groups or patterns of criminal activity, plus performing related duties as assigned. The position may entail testifying in court and traveling to perform certain work functions.

Qualifications:
An entry level position requires three years of experience with a criminal justice, military, or government intelligence agency or criminal intelligence network organization, or in a business, financial, or academic environment compiling data, analyzing findings and writing reports. A bachelor's degree in criminal justice or related field may substitute for two years of experience. The position may require obtaining and maintaining top-secret clearances.

Education:
A minimum high school diploma or General Education Diploma or equivalent experience is required for this position. Applicants should be aware that more education increases the likelihood of promotion and advancement.

Preferred/Required Skills:
1.   Effective oral and writing skills
2.   Good interpersonal skills
3.   Good problem solving ability
4.   Good judgment in safeguarding sensitive information
5.   Good computer skills for data analysis and records management
6.   Ability to create extremely accurate, detailed reports
7.   Ability to work independently, as well as in a team

Training:
No specific agency/state training noted.

Grade Level(s): 2015

What to Expect:
1. Employment history check
2. Criminal history check
3. Drug use history check
4. Personal history check
5. Applicant may encounter a waiting period
6. May involve drug testing

Salary Range:
The salary range for this position is $38,000 to $51,000 per year.

*This example is for Arizona. Salary and qualifications may vary by state.

Deputy Chief Clerk IV JG-28

Description:
Deputy Chief Clerks IV are the second highest ranking non-judicial employees in Supreme and County, City, Family and Surrogate Courts. They serve in a confidential capacity and are responsible for managing court operations related to case processing, budget and payroll preparation, deployment and management of non-judicial personnel, coordination with non-court agencies, and other related duties.

Qualifications:
Applicants must have a bachelor's degree from an accredited college or university and three years of work experience involving managerial responsibilities, or an equivalent combination of experience and education.

Education:
A minimum bachelor's degree is required for this position.

Preferred/Required Skills:
1. Managerial skills
2. Knowledge of court system
3. Interpersonal skills

Training:
No specific agency/state training noted.

Grade Level(s): JG-28

What to Expect:
1. Employment history check
2. Interview

Salary Range:
The minimum salary for this position is $68,125 plus $1,200 location pay per year.

*This example is for New York State. Salary and qualifications may vary by state and agency.

Highway Patrol (Commander): Department of Public Safety

Description:
The position entails commanding a major segment or function of the Department of Public Safety. Responsibilities include coordinating, planning, supervising, and evaluating the work of assigned personnel within an operational or support function. Supervision is exercised over a staff of sworn and/or civilian personnel primarily through subordinate supervisors. Commanders perform a variety of complex administrative duties, and related duties, as required. The position may require response to crime scenes or critical incidents and exposure to outdoor weather conditions, fumes or dust, toxic or caustic chemicals or bodily fluids.

Qualifications:
Applicants must have three years of experience and permanent status as a Lieutenant. Applicants must have an overall performance evaluation rating of at least "standard" for the preceding 12 months. One hundred twenty semester hours from an accredited college or university may substitute for one year of experience, and applicants must successfully complete the examination process.

Education:
A minimum high school diploma or General Education Diploma is required for this position. Applicants should be aware that more education increases the likelihood of promotion and advancement.

Preferred/Required Skills:
1.   Effective oral and writing skills
2.   Good interpersonal skills
3.   Good problem solving ability
4.   Good judgment
5.   Self-control
6.   Bilingualism is a plus, especially in Spanish
7.   Sound mental and physical health

Training:
No specific agency/state training noted.

Grade Level(s): 1266

What to Expect:
1.   Employment history check
2.   Criminal history check
3.   Drug use history check
4.   Personal history check
5.   Applicant may encounter a waiting period
6.   May involve drug testing
7.   Medical examination

Salary Range:
The starting salary for this position is $90,000 per year.

*This example is for Arizona. Salary and qualifications may vary from state to state.

Highway Patrol Officer (Cadet): Department of Public Safety

Description:
Highway Patrol Officers patrol the roadways of the state providing protection to the public through diligent enforcement of all traffic laws and other statutes. In performing this function, they investigate traffic collisions, direct and control traffic, apprehend violators, promote highway safety, and assist other law enforcement agencies.

Qualifications:
Applicants must be citizens of the U.S., possess a high school diploma or General Education Diploma, be at least 21 years of age at the time of graduation from the academy, and possess a valid driver's license.

Education:
A minimum high school diploma or General Education Diploma is required for this position. Applicants should be aware that more education increases the likelihood of promotion and advancement.

Preferred/Required Skills:
1. Good interpersonal skills
2. Effective oral and written communication skills
3. Good problem solving ability
4. Good judgment
5. Self-control
.6. Bilingualism, especially in Spanish, is a plus
7. Sound mental and physical health

Training:
The Cadet Officer participates in an academy training program to learn the general duties of police work. Upon graduation from the academy, the Cadet Officer is promoted to Officer and attends an advanced basic training program.

Grade Level(s): Not applicable

What to Expect:
1. Employment history check
2. Criminal history check
3. Drug use history check
4. Personal history check
5. Applicant may encounter a waiting period
6. May involve drug testing
7. Medical examination

Salary Range:
The salary range for this position is $36,000 to $47,000 per year.

*This example is for Arizona. Salary and qualifications may vary by state.

Intelligence Research Specialist: Department of Public Safety

Description:
Intelligence Research Specialists research, obtain, interpret, and disseminate confidential investigative intelligence information upon request in direct support of the investigative operations for various law enforcement agencies or criminal information networks. They ensure that information obtained is accurate and released only to authorized personnel. They make oral presentations to individuals or groups to disseminate information. They perform related duties as assigned.

Qualifications:
An entry level position requires two years of experience with a law enforcement or criminal justice agency as a police records clerk or dispatcher, or performing investigative research. Two years of college education in criminal justice or related field may substitute for one year of experience. One year of the experience must be in a computer database system. The position requires knowledge of records management systems; research techniques; federal and state laws related to assignment; and law enforcement and intelligence terminology.

Education:
A minimum associate's degree is preferred, but a high school diploma or General Education Diploma is acceptable for this position. More education increases the likelihood of promotion and advancement.

Preferred/Required Skills:
1. Effective oral and writing skills
2. Effective listening techniques
3. Performing detailed work with a high degree of accuracy
4. Ability to work under stressful or changing conditions
5. Ability to work independently or in a team
6. Exercise good judgment in safeguarding information
7. Establish and maintain effective working relationships with others

Training:
No specific agency/state training noted.

Grade Level(s): 2005

What to Expect:
1.   Employment history check
2.   Criminal history check
3.   Drug use history check
4.   Personal history check
5.   Applicant may encounter a waiting period
6.   May involve drug testing
7.   May involve medical examination

Salary Range:
The salary range for this position is $29,000 to $39,000 per year.

*This example is for Arizona. Salary and qualifications may vary by state.

Investigator Trainee: Department of Alcoholic Beverage Control

Description:
Investigators are non-uniformed, sworn peace officers who perform the full range of peace officer duties and responsibilities in the accomplishment of their assignments. Their duties include determining suitability for license of those who wish to be licensed to manufacture, transport and sell alcoholic beverages within the state; conduct investigations to detect or verify suspected violations of provisions of all federal, state, county, and city laws in and about licensed premises; locate and interview accused persons and witnesses; gather evidence; make arrests; appear as witnesses; serve legal papers; and other duties related to their position.

Qualifications:
Minimum qualifications for this position include the equivalent of two years of college with a major in police science, administration of justice, criminal justice, criminology, public administration, law enforcement, or auditing.

Education:
This position requires a minimum associate's degree . Applicants should be aware that more education increases the likelihood of promotion and advancement.

Preferred/Required Skills:
1. Interpersonal skills
2. Investigative skills
3. Writing skills

Training:
Trainees must successfully complete all required training.

Grade Level(s): Investigator Trainee

What to Expect:
1. Employment history check
2. Background investigation
3. Written test
4. Interview

Salary Range:
The salary range for this position as a trainee is $30,000 to $34,000 per year.

*This example is for California. Salary and qualifications may vary by state and agency.

Polygraph Examiner: Department of Public Safety

Description:
Polygraph examiners administer polygraph examinations for employment screening, internal investigations, and criminal cases. They read and interpret polygraph chart responses in order to determine the results of the examinations; prepare polygraph reports; supervise the work and training of part-time examiners; communicate with law enforcement agencies throughout the state; review and update policies and procedures related to the unit; prepare monthly and quarterly reports; provide expert testimony in court; and perform related duties as assigned.

Qualifications:
An entry level position requires successful completion of approved polygraph course work and three years of experience in criminal investigation or polygraph administration. The position requires

knowledge of applied psychology and physiology relevant to polygraph testing; constitutional rights of persons regarding confessions; and criminal investigative procedures.

Education:
A minimum high school diploma or General Education Diploma is required for this position. More education may increase the likelihood of promotion and advancement.

Preferred/Required Skills:
1.   Effective oral and writing skills
2.   Good interpersonal skills
3.   Interrogation and interviewing skills
4.   Good judgment
5.   Bilingualism, especially in Spanish, is a plus

Training:
No specific agency/state training noted.

Grade Level(s): 9724

What to Expect:
1.   Employment history check
2.   Criminal history check
3.   Drug use history check
4.   Personal history check
5.   Applicant may encounter a waiting period
6.   May involve drug testing

Salary Range:
The salary range for this position is $42,000 to $57,000 per year.

*This example is for Arizona. Salary and qualifications may vary by state.

Probation Officer and Correctional Treatment Specialist – Juvenile

Description:
The position provides case management services, and individual and group counseling to resident clients. The work setting is an office or lodge

in a juvenile correctional facility and entails some risk from juvenile actions. Some travel is required.

Qualifications:
Four years providing counseling, casework, education and/or supervision to clients in a correctional setting is required for this position. College education in any field may substitute for two years of experience. Applicants must possess and maintain a valid driver's license, and pass a background check and pre-employment physical exam.

Education:
The position requires fifteen semester hours in psychology, criminology, penology, sociology, guidance and counseling and/or social work. Applicants should be aware that more education increases the likelihood of promotion and advancement.

Preferred/Required Skills:
1.   Excellent interpersonal skills
2.   Counseling skills
3.   Ability to work independently as well as in a team
4.   Effective writing skills

Training:
No specific agency/state training noted.

Grade Level(s): Not applicable

What to Expect:
1.   Employment history check
2.   Background criminal check
3.   Pre-employment physical exam

Salary Range:
The salary range for this position is $24,000 to $44,000 per year.

*This example is for New Mexico. Salary and qualifications may vary by state.

Security Officer: Department of Public Safety

Description:
Under general supervision, Security Officers provide armed security for buildings and property. Security Officers control visitor and employee access; screen packages and mail; monitor security cameras; monitor alarm systems; prepare incident reports; patrol buildings and grounds; maintain proficiency in the use of weapons and equipment; provide training to new security personnel; provide crowd and traffic control as needed; and perform other duties as required.

Qualifications:
An entry level position requires one year of experience as a security officer, military police officer or law enforcement officer involving public contact. Applicants must have a valid driver's license and must successfully complete the examination process.

Education:
A minimum high school diploma or General Education Diploma is required for this position. Applicants should be aware that more education increases the likelihood of promotion and advancement.

Preferred/Required Skills:
1.   Effective oral and writing skills
2.   Good interpersonal skills
3.   Interpret and act upon moderately difficult written information
4.   Work effectively under highly stressful conditions
5.   Ability to work independently with minimal supervision, as well as in a team
6.   Ability to rapidly prioritize a variety of tasks and take appropriate action
7.   Ability to apply first responder techniques in performing emergency first aid

Training:
No specific agency/state training noted.

Grade Level(s): 6101

What to Expect:
1.   Employment history check
2.   Criminal history check
3.   Drug use history check
4.   Personal history check
5.   Applicant may encounter a waiting period
6.   May involve drug testing

Salary Range:
The salary range for this position is $26,000 to $36,000 per year.

*This example is for Arizona. Salary and qualifications may vary by state.

Security Supervisor: Department of Public Safety

Description:
Under direction, Security Supervisors perform work of considerable responsibility in planning and directing a 24-hour security operation and armed security staff. They train subordinate personnel; conduct inspections; identify potential security problem areas and provide technical advice; and perform other duties as required.

Qualifications:
An entry level position requires two years experience as a Department of Public Safety Security Officer or three years of experience as a security officer, military police officer or law enforcement officer involving public contact. Applicants must successfully complete the examination process and must have a valid driver's license.

Education:
A minimum high school diploma or General Education Diploma is required for this position. Applicants should be aware that more education may increase the likelihood of promotion and advancement.

Preferred/Required Skills:
1.   Effective oral and writing skills
2.   Good interpersonal skills
3.   Interpret and act upon moderately difficult written information
4.   Work effectively under highly stressful conditions

5.   Ability to work independently with minimal supervision, as well as in a team
6.   Ability to rapidly prioritize a variety of tasks and take appropriate action
7.   Ability to apply first responder techniques in performing emergency first aid
8.   Ability to effectively supervise subordinates

Training:
No specific agency/state training noted.

Grade Level(s): 6102

What to Expect:
1.   Employment history check
2.   Criminal history check
3.   Drug use history check
4.   Personal history check
5.   Applicant may encounter a waiting period
6.   May involve drug testing
7.   May involve medical examination

Salary Range:
The salary range for this position is $39,000 to $53,000 per year.

*This example is for Arizona. Salary and qualifications may vary by state.

Senior Police Communications Dispatcher: Department of Public Safety

Description:
Under limited supervision, a Senior Police Communications Dispatcher simultaneously operates a multi-channel radio console, computer terminal and multi-line telephone while maintaining written logs and records; receives, coordinates and disseminates critical information from various sources; serves as acting shift supervisor when needed, and provides on-the-job training to new Police Communications Dispatchers. The position may also entail serving as a training coordinator responsible for classroom instruction of new Police Communications Dispatchers, as well as on-

going training of existing dispatchers. Travel on a limited basis may be required. This position involves working irregular hours, holidays, and weekends.

Qualifications:
At the entry level, the position requires three years of experience as a Police Communications Dispatcher with the Department of Public Safety, or three years of police dispatching experience, including one year as a dispatcher with the Department of Public Safety.

Education:
The position requires a minimum high school diploma or General Education Diploma. Applicants should be aware that more education increases the likelihood of promotion and advancement.

Preferred/Required Skills:
1.   Effective oral and writing skills
2.   Good interpersonal skills
3.   Ability to plan, organize, coordinate and implement training programs for dispatcher trainees, dispatchers, and officers.
4.   Ability to develop, lead, and participate in teams and work groups
5.   Ability to perform research and develop written training materials
6.   Skilled in decision-making/problem-solving in crisis or emergency situations
7.   Ability to effectively interpret a variety of maps and dispatch information to field personnel

Training:
No specific agency/state training noted.

Grade Level(s): 6305

What to Expect:
1.   Employment history check
2.   Criminal history check
3.   Drug use history check
4.   Personal history check
5.   Applicant may encounter a waiting period
6.   May involve drug testing

Salary Range:
The salary range for this position is $35,000 to $48,000 per year.

*This example is for Arizona. Salary and qualifications may vary by state.

Sergeant: Department of Public Safety

Description:
Sergeants supervise police officers and/or civilian employees engaged in the performance of highway patrol, criminal investigations, or other related police operations. Sergeants plan, schedule, coordinate, supervise, and evaluate the work of sworn officers and civilian personnel. They may be required to respond to crime scenes or critical incidents and may be exposed to outdoor weather conditions. Sergeants testify in court, and direct investigations into citizen or internal complaints against employees of the department. They may be assigned to an administrative staff position without supervisory responsibilities.

Qualifications:
The position requires four years of experience and permanent status with the Department of Public Safety as a sworn peace officer in the classification of Officer or Pilot. Applicants must have an overall performance evaluation rating of at least "standard" for the last twelve months and must successfully complete the examination process.

Education:
A minimum high school diploma or General Education Diploma is required for this position. Applicants should be aware that more education increases the likelihood of promotion and advancement.

Preferred/Required Skills:
1.   Effective oral and writing skills
2.   Good interpersonal skills
3.   Ability to analyze situations under stressful conditions and adopt effective courses of action
4.   Good judgment
5.   Ability to effectively supervise subordinates
6.   Ability to work with other law enforcement agencies in planning and coordinating task force operations, special events, and activities

Training:
No specific agency/state training noted.

Grade Level(s): 1241

What to Expect:
1.   Employment history check
2.   Criminal history check
3.   Drug use history check
4.   Personal history check
5.   Applicant may encounter a waiting period
6.   May involve drug testing
7.   May involve medical examination

Salary Range:
The minimum salary for this position is $52,000 per year.

*This example is for Arizona. Salary and qualifications may vary by state.

Social and Community Service Coordinator (Caseworker) – Juvenile

Description:
Caseworkers investigate or accept and process reports of allegations of adult/child abuse and neglect. Caseworkers perform their duties in the office, client's homes, or institutions. Some travel may be required. Risk from hostile clients is possible.

Qualifications:
Applicants must have a bachelor's degree in social work, criminal justice, counseling, psychology, family services, or education from an accredited college or university. A current and valid driver's license is required.

Education:
A bachelor's degree is required for this position. Applicants should be aware that more education increases the likelihood of promotion and advancement.

Preferred/Required Skills:
1.   Excellent interpersonal skills

2.   Counseling skills
3.   Ability to work independently as well as in a team
4.   Effective writing skills

Training:
All required agency/state training must be successfully completed.

Grade Level(s): Not applicable

What to Expect:
1.   Employment history check
2.   Criminal history check
3.   Interview

Salary Range:
The salary range for this position is $24,000 to $42,000 annually.

*This example is for New Mexico. Salary and qualifications may vary by state.

State Trooper

Description:
State troopers perform general law enforcement duties, as well as patrol highways.

Qualifications:
Applicants must be U.S. citizens, at least 18 years of age, and possess a valid driver's license. Applicants must possess a two or four year degree in law enforcement or criminal justice. In Minnesota, the applicant must possess a valid Minnesota State Peace Officer's license.

Education:
Applicants must possess a two or four year degree in law enforcement or criminal justice. Applicants should be aware that more education increases the likelihood of promotion and advancement.

Preferred/Required Skills:
1.   Effective oral and writing skills

2. Good interpersonal skills
3. Good problem solving ability
4. Good judgment
5. Self-control
6. Bilingualism is a plus
7. Sound mental and physical health

Training:
If hired, the applicant must successfully complete several months of training.

Grade Level(s): Not applicable

What to Expect:
1. Employment history check
2. Criminal history check
3. Drug use history check
4. Personal history check
5. Applicant may encounter a waiting period
6. May involve drug testing
7. May involve a medical examination

Salary Range:
The salary range for this position is $39,000 to $52,000 per year.

*This example is for Minnesota. Salary and qualifications may vary by state.

FEDERAL POSITIONS

Adjudicator (Starting Position): Office of Security, Central Intelligence Agency

Description:
It is the function of the CIA to provide timely, reliable, and useful information to the President of the United States and national policy makers. Within this larger mission, it is the role of the Office of Security to provide a comprehensive, world wide security program that protects Agency personnel, programs, information, facilities, and activities.

Adjudicators use information gathered by investigators to assess and make final recommendations in an analytical report format. Additional disciplines in the Office of Security include specialized investigations, risk assessments, polygraph operations, analytical adjudications, physical security, and information systems security.

Qualifications:
Applicant (both self and spouse) must have U.S. citizenship and must successfully complete a thorough screening process to include intellectual and personality screening, a writing test, and interviews. They must also undergo a complete background investigation and medical screening prior to final employment. A college degree with a 3.0/4.0 GPA is required. All positions require relocation to the Washington D.C. metropolitan area.

Education:
A bachelor's degree is required for this position. Applicants should be aware that more education may allow the applicant to start at a higher grade level, and increases the likelihood of promotion and advancement.

Preferred/Required Skills:
1.   Effective oral and writing skills
2.   Good interpersonal skills
3.   Analytical skills
4.   High levels of trustworthiness, integrity, and loyalty to the U.S.

Training:
Security Officers are trained through a system of formal training courses and rotational assignments that provide exposure to a wide variety of security disciplines.

Grade Level(s): Not listed

What to Expect:
1.   Intellectual screening
2.   Personality screening
3.   Medical screening
4.   Background investigation
5.   Writing test
6.   Interviews
7.   Applicant may encounter a waiting period

Salary Range:
The salary range for this position is $30,000 to $50,000 per year depending on qualifications, education, and experience.

Border Patrol Agent: Department of Homeland Security, Bureau of Citizenship and Immigration Services

Description:
Border Patrol Agents are responsible for detecting and preventing illegal entry and illegal smuggling into the United States. Border Patrol Agents apprehend illegal aliens and smugglers of aliens at or near land borders. Border Patrol Agents use many techniques to aid them, such as following tracks, marks and other evidence; maintaining surveillance; electronic signaling devices; following leads; and aircraft sightings; etc.

Qualifications:
Applicants must be U.S. citizens, less than 37 years of age, and possess a valid state driver's license. Applicants must pass a background investigation, physical exam, and oral interview. Applicants must possess substantial law enforcement experience or must possess completion of a bachelor's degree from an accredited college or university. Proficiency in another language is valued.

Education:
A minimum high school diploma or General Education Diploma is required for this position, depending on experience. Applicants should be aware that more education increases the likelihood of promotion and advancement.

Preferred/Required Skills:
1.   Effective oral and writing skills
2.   Good interpersonal skills
3.   Good problem solving ability
4.   Good judgment
5.   Self-control
6.   Bilingualism, especially in Spanish and Middle Eastern languages
7.   Sound mental and physical health

Training:
Border Patrol Agents must successfully complete 18 weeks of training at the Border Patrol Academy located at the Federal Law Enforcement Training Center, Glynco, Georgia.

Grade Level(s): GS-5 through GS-7

What to Expect:
1. Interview
2. Physical exam
3. Background investigation
4. Applicant may encounter a waiting period

Salary Range:
The salary range for this position is $23,000 to $37,000 per year.

Civil Aviation Security Specialist (Federal Air Marshal): Department of Transportation, Federal Aviation Administration (FAA)

Description:
Federal Air Marshals (FAMs) respond to criminal incidents aboard U.S. air carriers, as well as other in-flight emergencies. FAMs are authorized to carry firearms and make arrests, while preserving the safety of aircraft, crew, and passengers. FAMs perform regular and extended travel, both foreign and domestic, for several weeks at a time. They work irregular hours and shifts, and are on call 24 hours per day. While deployed, they have limited personal contact with family and limited time off. FAMs travel to and spend time in foreign countries that are sometimes politically or economically unstable and may pose a high probability of terrorist or criminal activity against the U.S. Government. Federal Air Marshal bases are assigned throughout the country at major metropolitan areas.

Qualifications:
Applicants must be U.S. citizens and under 40 years of age. Previous experience in a covered Federal law enforcement position may exempt candidates from this age requirement. Applicants must have at least three years of general experience or a bachelor's degree. Federal Air Marshals must be eligible for and maintain a top secret security clearance based upon a favorably adjudicated special background investigation as a

condition of employment. FAMs are subject to drug and alcohol testing, random, and as needed. FAMs are required to maintain firearms certification and to participate in all elements of the FAM physical fitness program. FAMs are required to have annual wellness physicals to meet and maintain medical standards.

Education:
A bachelor's degree or equivalent experience is required for this position. Applicants should be aware that more education increases the likelihood of promotion and advancement.

Preferred/Required Skills:
1. Effective oral and writing skills
2. Good interpersonal skills
3. Good problem solving ability
4. Good judgment
5. Self-control

Training:
Candidates hired into FAM positions must successfully complete FMTP Blocks 1,2,3, and 4 of the Federal Air Marshal Training Program (FAMTP) conducted by the Federal Law Enforcement Training Center (FLETC) in Glynco, Georgia and the FAA to remain eligible for the position.

Grade Level(s): FV-G, FV-H, FV-I

What to Expect:
1. Background investigation
2. Physical exam
3. Medical exam
4. Drug and alcohol testing
5. Applicant may encounter a waiting period

Salary Range:
The salary range for this position is $35,100-$80,800 per year.

Contract Linguist: Department of Justice, Federal Bureau of Investigation

Description:
The FBI has opportunities for Contract Linguists in many major U.S. metropolitan areas. These opportunities include various types of language-related services such as interpreting, testing, monitoring, and translation. FBI Contract Linguists primarily perform document-to-document or audio-to-document translation services on any subject matter for which the FBI has jurisdiction. Contract Linguists are self-employed and do not receive benefits.

Qualifications:
Consideration is currently being afforded English-speaking candidates with a professional level of language fluency in Amharic, Azerbaijani, Berber, Chinese, German, Hebrew, Hindi, Indonesian, Japanese, Kazakh, Korean, Malay, Pashto, Punjabi, Somali, Tagalog, Tamil, Turkish, Turkmen, Urdu, Uzbek, Vietnamese, and Yiddish. The minimum qualifications include United States citizenship; residence within the U.S. for at least three out of the last five years; ability to pass a battery of language proficiency tests, polygraph examination; and a 10-year scope background investigation. Language needs may change with the FBI's area of interest.

Education:
A minimum high school diploma or General Education Diploma is required for this position.

Preferred/Required Skills:
1.   Excellent translation skills

Training:
No specific agency/state training noted.

Grade Level(s): Independent Contractor

What to Expect:
1.   Language proficiency tests
2.   Background investigation
3.   Polygraph testing

Salary Range:
This is not a salaried position. Contract Linguists are paid an hourly rate of $24 to $38 per hour, depending on the language.

Contract Monitor: Department of Justice, Federal Bureau of Investigation

Description:
The FBI has opportunities for Contract Monitors in many major U.S. metropolitan areas. These opportunities include various types of language-related services such as interpreting, testing, monitoring, and translating. Contract Monitors perform summary translations of voice recordings. The subject matter maybe in any area for which the FBI has jurisdiction. FBI Contract Monitors are self-employed and do not receive benefits.

Qualifications:
Consideration is currently being afforded English-speaking candidates with a professional level of language fluency in Amharic, Azerbaijani, Berber, Chinese, German, Hebrew, Hindi, Indonesian, Japanese, Kazakh, Korean, Malay, Pashto, Punjabi, Somali, Tagalog, Tamil, Turkish, Turkmen, Urdu, Uzbek, Vietnamese, and Yiddish. Minimum qualifications include United States citizenship; residence within the U.S. for at least three out of the last five years; ability to pass a battery of language proficiency tests, polygraph examination, and a 10-year scope background investigation.

Education:
A minimum high school diploma or General Education Diploma is required for this position.

Preferred/Required Skills:
1.   Excellent translation skills

Training:
No specific agency/state training noted.

Grade Level(s): Independent Contractor

What to Expect:
1.   Language proficiency tests
2.   Background investigation
3.   Polygraph testing

Salary Range:
This is not a salaried position. Contract Monitors are paid an hourly rate of $24 to $38 per hour, depending on the language.

Contract Tester: Department of Justice, Federal Bureau of Investigation

Description:
The FBI has opportunities for Contract Testers in many major U.S. metropolitan areas. Contract Testers provide oral and written testing services for the purposes of determining the language ability of potential FBI employees, contractors, and on-board employees in English and the target language. Because of the evaluative nature of this position, expert level proficiency is required. FBI Contract Testers are self-employed and do not receive benefits.

Qualifications:
Consideration is currently being afforded English-speaking candidates with a professional level of language fluency in Amharic, Azerbaijani, Berber, Chinese, German, Hebrew, Hindi, Indonesian, Japanese, Kazakh, Korean, Malay, Pashto, Punjabi, Somali, Tagalog, Tamil, Turkish, Turkmen, Urdu, Uzbek, Vietnamese, and Yiddish. Minimum qualifications include United States citizenship; residence within the U.S. for at least three out of the last five years; ability to pass a battery of language proficiency tests, polygraph examination, and a 10-year scope background investigation.

Education:
A minimum high school diploma or General Education Diploma is required for this position.

Preferred/Required Skills:
1.   Expert language skills
2.   Good interpersonal skills

3.   Effective oral and writing skills

Training:
No specific agency/state training noted.

Grade Level(s): Independent Contractor

What to Expect:
1.   Language proficiency tests
2.   Background investigation
3.   Polygraph testing

Salary Range:
This is not a salaried position. Contract Testers are paid an hourly rate of $24 to $38 per hour, depending on the language.

Correctional Officer: Bureau of Prisons

Description:
Correctional Officers enforce the regulations governing the operation of a correctional institution, serving both as a supervisor and counselor of inmates.

Qualifications:
To qualify at the GS-05 grade level, applicants must have successfully completed a bachelor's degree from an accredited college or university, or a combination of undergraduate education and experience equivalent to three years of full-time experience. To qualify at the GS-06 grade level, applicants must have nine semester hours of graduate study in criminal justice, criminology, social science, or a related field, or the equivalent of at least one year of full-time specialized experience. Combinations of education and experience are acceptable, as well as pertinent volunteer experience.

Education:
Applicants must have at least a bachelor's degree in criminal justice or a related field. Applicants should be aware that more education increases the likelihood of promotion and advancement.

Preferred/Required Skills:
1. Excellent interpersonal skills
2. Ability to effectively interact with diverse cultures
3. Good self-control and judgment

Training:
Trainees must successfully complete training at Glynco, Georgia.

Grade Level(s): GS-007-05 to GS-007-06

What to Expect:
1. Background check
2. Interview

Salary Range:
The salary range for this position is $23,000 to $34,000 per year.

Correctional Treatment Specialist: Bureau of Prisons

Description:
Correctional Treatment Specialists perform correctional casework in an institutional setting; develop, evaluate and analyze program needs and other data about inmates; evaluate progress of individual offenders in the institution; coordinate and integrate inmate training programs; develop social histories; evaluate positive and negative aspects in each case situation; and develop parole and release plans.

Qualifications:
Applicants must have a bachelor's degree from an accredited college or university that includes at least 24 hours in the behavioral or social sciences, such as correctional administration, criminal justice, sociology, or a related field, or a combination of education and experience that includes at least 24 hours in the behavioral or social sciences. In addition to the basic qualifications, applicants at the GS-09 level must have a master's degree or possess one year of specialized experience equivalent to at least the GS-07 level that was gained in casework in a correctional institution or in another criminal justice setting, or counseling experience. Applicants at the GS-11 level must possess the basic qualifications, as well as three years of progressively higher level graduate education leading to

a Ph.D. or one year of specialized experience equivalent to at least the GS-09 level.

Education:
Applicants must have at least a bachelor's degree. More education and experience may allow the applicant to start at a higher level and increases the likelihood of promotion and advancement.

Preferred/Required Skills:
1.   Counseling skills
2.   Excellent interpersonal skills
3.   Organizational skills
4.   Good writing skills

Training:
Trainees must successfully complete all agency/state required training.

Grade Level(s): GS-101-09 to GS-101-11

What to Expect:
1.   Interview

Salary Range:
The salary range for this position is $35,000 to $55,000 per year.

Criminal Investigator (Special Agent): Department of Homeland Security, Bureau of Citizenship and Immigration Services (BCIS)

Description:
Criminal Investigators plan and conduct investigations, often undercover, concerning possible violations of criminal and administrative provisions of the Immigration and Nationality Act and other statutes under the United States Code. These officers carry firearms, make arrests, prepare investigative reports, present cases to the United States Attorneys for prosecution, and give testimony in judicial and administrative proceedings. They maintain liaison and work closely with federal, state, and local agencies. Criminal Investigators are located throughout the United States, including Guam, Puerto Rico, and the Virgin Islands. Most positions are located in metropolitan areas which have larger offices.

Qualifications:
Applicants must be U.S. citizens, possess a valid state driver's license, pass a written test, physical exam and background investigation. In addition, candidates must have, for three of the last five years immediately before applying for the position (1) resided in the U.S.; or (2) worked in the United States Government as an employee overseas in a federal or military capacity; or (3) been a dependent of a U.S. federal or military employee serving overseas. Applicants must be under 37 years of age. Applicants must have three years of progressively responsible law enforcement experience or possess a bachelor's degree in any field from an accredited college or university, or possess a combination of qualifying education and experience.

Education:
A bachelor's degree or an acceptable combination of education and experience is required for this position. Applicants should be aware that more education increases the likelihood of promotion and advancement.

Preferred/Required Skills:
1.   Effective oral and writing skills
2.   Good interpersonal skills
3.   Good problem solving ability
4.   Good judgment
5.   Self-control
6.   Bilingualism in Spanish is a plus

Training:
Criminal Investigators (Special Agents) will receive a 14 to 18 week Immigration Officer's Basic Training Course at one of the Service's training centers and pass a course of study in immigration law, nationality law, Spanish language, police training, and branch specific operational training.

Grade Level(s): GS-5 through GS-12

What to Expect:
1.   Written test
2.   Physical test
3.   Background investigation

Salary Range:
The salary range for this position is $23,000 to $66,000 per year.

Criminal Investigator: Department of the Interior, Bureau of Indian Affairs

Description:
Criminal Investigators are involved with planning and conducting investigations relating to alleged and/or suspected violations of the law, program or property abuse on Indian Reservations and/or Indian owned land within the Bureau of Indian Affairs jurisdiction. These positions require a primary knowledge of investigative techniques and a knowledge of laws and evidence, rules of criminal procedure, precedent court decisions concerning admissibility of evidence, and search and seizure related issues. Criminal Investigators cooperate with other federal, state, and local agencies looking for those who live on Indian lands. Criminal Investigators may be called upon to do surveillance and/or undercover work.

Qualifications:
Applicants must be U.S. citizens and must be between 21 and 37 years of age. They must possess a valid driver's license and pass a background investigation. Knowledge of federal, state, and local laws or investigative experience is preferred. Applicants must also have a bachelor's degree from an accredited college or university.

Education:
A bachelor's degree is required for this position. Applicants should be aware that more education increases the likelihood of promotion and advancement.

Preferred/Required Skills:
1. Effective oral and writing skills
2. Good interpersonal skills
3. Good problem solving ability
4. Good judgment
5. Self-control

Training:
Criminal Investigators will attend a nine week training school at the Federal Law Enforcement Training Center at Glynco, Georgia.

Grade Level(s): GS-5 through GS-7

What to Expect:
1. Interview
2. Background investigation

Salary Range:
The salary range for this position is $23,000 to $37,000 per year.

Criminal Investigator: Department of the Interior, Bureau of Land Management

Description:
Criminal Investigators are involved with the planning and conducting of investigations relating to alleged and/or suspected violations of the law, and program or property abuse on federally-owned public lands consisting of forests and ranges under the jurisdiction of the Bureau of Land Management. These positions require a primary knowledge of investigative techniques and a knowledge of laws and evidence, rules of criminal procedure, precedent court decisions concerning admissibility of evidence and search and seizure related issues. Criminal Investigators investigate crimes, such as natural resource crimes (i.e.: illegal removal of), archeological crimes (i.e.: theft or destruction of) within the BLM's jurisdiction. Criminal Investigators cooperate with other federal, state, and local agencies. Bureau of Land Management Criminal Investigators also are involved with operating drug eradication programs.

Qualifications:
Applicants must be U.S. citizens, be between the ages of 21 and 37, possess a valid driver's license, pass a background investigation, and pass a physical examination. Applicants with a knowledge of federal, state, and local laws or investigative experience are preferred. Applicants must possess completion of a bachelor's degree from an accredited college or university or possess an appropriate amount of experience.

Education:
A bachelor's degree is required for this position. An acceptable amount of experience may substitute for education. Applicants should be aware that more education increases the likelihood of promotion and advancement.

Preferred/Required Skills:
1. Effective oral and writing skills
2. Good interpersonal skills
3. Good problem solving ability
4. Investigative skills

Training:
Criminal Investigators will attend a nine week training school at the Federal Law Enforcement Training Center at Glynco, Georgia.

Grade Level(s): GS-9 through GS-13

What to Expect:
1. Background investigation
2. Physical exam
3. Applicant may encounter a waiting period

Salary Range:
The salary range for this position is $35,000 to $79,000 per year.

Customs Enforcement Instructor: Department of the Treasury, U.S. Customs Service

Description:
This position is located at the Office of Training and Development, U.S. Customs Academy at the Federal Law Enforcement Academy (FLETC) in Glynco, Georgia. Customs Enforcement Instructors design, develop, revise, conduct, and evaluate new training programs to determine the most effective method of meeting Customs training objectives. They serve as advisors to the U.S. Customs Service Academy at Headquarters, providing professional and technical information and advice on training techniques.

Qualifications:
Applicants must have one year of specialized experience equivalent to the

next lower grade level, which has equipped the applicant with the particular knowledge, skills, and abilities to successfully perform the duties of the position, and that is typically in or related to the work of the position. Applicants must pass a physical exam, drug testing, and background investigation. After meeting all minimum application requirements, applicants are rated and ranked on the basis of experience, training, and awards received.

Education:
A minimum high school diploma or General Education Diploma, or equivalent experience is required. Applicants should be aware that more education increases the likelihood of promotion and advancement.

Preferred/Required Skills:
1. Effective oral and writing skills
2. Ability to prepare formal presentations
3. Knowledge of instructional techniques
4. Ability develop written material of an instructional nature
5. Knowledge of Federal and Customs investigative or inspectional laws, regulations, policies, procedures, and practices

Training:
No specific agency/state training noted.

Grade Level(s): GS-1801

What to Expect:
1. Background investigation
2. Physical exam
3. Drug testing

Salary Range:
The salary range for this position is $64,000 to $83,000 per year.

Customs Patrol Officer: Department of the Treasury, U.S. Customs Service

Description:
Customs Patrol Officers enforce customs and related laws through pre-

interdictory investigations and comprehensive tactical operations. They identify, locate, intercept, apprehend, and participate in the prosecution of individuals involved in organized smuggling of contraband and merchandise into the U.S.. Customs Patrol Officers utilize a full range of investigative techniques including interviews, interrogations, research of records and documents, and informants. They secure air support from Customs Air Support Branch and/or state or local agencies, and may fly as an observer to locate and identify suspects. Frequent travel may be required, and the position requires carrying a firearm and maintaining firearm proficiency.

Qualifications:
Applicants must be Native Americans who possess tribal certification that indicates one-fourth or more Indian blood. A copy of the certification must be submitted with the application package. Applicants must not have reached their 37th birthday, and must have a bachelor's degree from an accredited college or university. A combination of education and experience may qualify the applicant for the position. Applicants must have one year of specialized experience equivalent to the next lower grade, in or related to the work of the position described. Applicants must pass a pre-employment medical examination, drug screening, and background investigation.

Education:
A bachelor's degree or an acceptable combination of education and experience is required for this job. Applicants should be aware that more education increases the likelihood of promotion and advancement.

Preferred/Required Skills:
1. Effective oral and writing skills
2. Knowledge of law enforcement and criminal justice theories, techniques, procedures, and practices.
3. Good problem solving ability
4. Ability to apply various investigative techniques
5. Ability to develop and maintain sources of information

Training:
If hired, the applicant must successfully complete nine weeks of basic training at Glynco, Georgia.

Grade Level(s): GS-05, with potential to reach GS-11

What to Expect:
1. Background investigation
2. Medical exam
3. Drug testing
4. Applicant may encounter a waiting period

Salary Range:
The starting salary for this position is from $28,000 to $34,000 per year.

Deportation Officer: Department of Homeland Security, Bureau of Citizenship and Immigration Services

Description:
The Bureau of Citizenship and Immigration Services enforces our nation's laws regulating immigration and nationality matters. Under these laws, it may be necessary to detain and/or deport certain individuals. The mission of Deportation Officers is to provide for the control and removal of persons who have been ordered deported or otherwise required to depart from the U.S. Officers must closely monitor deportation proceedings from initiation to conclusion, which may require removal of an individual from the U.S. Close liaison with foreign consulates and embassies is required to facilitate the timely issuance of passports and travel documents required for deportation. Officers may be required to respond to Congressional inquiries. The majority of these positions are in district offices.

Qualifications:
Applicants must be U.S. citizens, possess a valid state driver's license, and pass a written test, physical exam and background investigation. In addition, candidates must have, for three of the last five years immediately before applying for the position (1) resided in the U.S.; or (2) worked in the United States Government as an employee overseas in a federal or military capacity; or (3) been a dependent of a U.S. federal or military employee serving overseas. Applicants must be under 37 years of age. Applicants must have three years of progressively responsible law enforcement experience or possess a bachelor's degree in any field from an accredited college or university, or possess a combination of qualifying education and experience.

Education:
A bachelor's degree or an acceptable combination of education and experience is required for this position.

Preferred/Required Skills:
1. Effective oral and writing skills
2. Good interpersonal skills
3. Good problem solving ability
4. Good judgment
5. Self-control
6. Bilingualism in Spanish is a plus

Training:
Immigration Deportation Officers will receive a 14 to 18 week Immigration Officer's Basic Training Course at one of the Service's training centers and must pass a course of study in immigration law, nationality law, Spanish language, police training, and branch specific operational training.

Grade Level(s): GS-5 through GS-12

What to Expect:
1. Written test
2. Physical exam
3. Background investigation
4. Applicant may encounter a waiting period

Salary Range:
The salary range for this position is $23,000 to $66,000 per year.

District Adjudications Officer (Center Adjudications Officer): Department of Homeland Security, Bureau of Citizenship and Immigration Services

Description:
Each year hundreds of people apply for various types of immigration benefits from the United States government. The benefits they seek include permission to import foreign workers, permission for relatives to immigrate, and permission to become American citizens. Adjudications

Officers determine eligibility for this wide variety of benefits. They review applications and often conduct interviews of the applicants. Adjudications Officers have the dual responsibility of providing courteous service to the public while being alert to the possibility of fraud and misrepresentation and usually perform duties in an office environment. District Adjudications Officers are located in the district offices nationwide. Center Adjudications Officers are located in the following Service Centers: St. Albans, VT; Lincoln, NE; Mesquite, TX; and Laguna Niguel, CA.

Qualifications:
Applicants must be U.S. citizens, possess a valid state driver's license, and must pass a written test and background investigation. In addition, candidates must have, for three of the last five years immediately before applying for the position (1) resided in the U.S.; or (2) worked in the United States Government as an employee overseas in a federal or military capacity; or (3) been a dependent of a U.S. federal or military employee serving overseas. Applicants must have three years of progressively responsible experience or possess a bachelor's degree in any field from an accredited college or university, or possess a combination of qualifying education and experience.

Education:
A bachelor's degree or an acceptable combination of education and experience is required for this position. Applicants should be aware that more education increases the likelihood of promotion and advancement.

Preferred/Required Skills:
1.   Effective oral and writing skills
2.   Good interpersonal skills
3.   Good problem solving ability
4.   Good judgment
5.   Self-control
6.   Bilingualism, especially in Spanish

Training:
Candidates selected for District Adjudications Officer and Center Adjudications Officer will be required initially to attend a 7 to 8 week Immigration Officer's Basic Course at a site close to their duty station, and pass a course of study in immigration and nationality law and branch

specific operational training, with possible courses in Spanish language and police training at an alternate site.

Grade Level(s): GS-5 through GS-12

What to Expect:
1. Written test
2. Physical exam
3. Background investigation
4. Applicant may encounter a waiting period

Salary Range:
The salary range for this position is $23,000 to $66,000 per year.

Diversion Investigator: Department of Justice, Drug Enforcement Administration (DEA)

Description:
Diversion Investigators are responsible for registering all manufacturers, distributors, and dispensers of controlled substances. Diversion Investigators are involved with auditing manufacturers and wholesalers, and the interdiction of any illegal diversion and distribution of illegal and dangerous drugs/narcotics.

Qualifications:
Applicants must be U.S. citizens; possess a valid driver's license; have a bachelor's degree with at least a "B" average; pass interviews, drug testing, medical examinations, and a thorough background investigation.

Education:
Applicants must have at least a bachelor's degree. Applicants should be aware that more education may allow the applicant to start at a higher level and increases the likelihood of promotion and advancement.

Preferred/Required Skills:
1. Effective oral and writing skills
2. Good interpersonal skills
3. Good problem solving ability
4. Good judgment

5. Self-control
6. Bilingualism is a plus
7. Sound mental and physical health

Training:
If hired, the applicant must successfully complete three months of training at the FBI academy campus in Quantico, VA.

Grade Level(s): GS-07 to GS-13

What to Expect:
1. Interviews
2. Background investigation
3. Medical exam
4. Drug testing
5. Applicant may encounter a waiting period

Salary Range:
The salary range for this position is $29,000 to $79,000 per year.

Foreign Service Officer: Department of State, Consular Affairs

Description:
The Department of State's highest priority is to protect American citizens who are residents or traveling abroad. Consular officers take the responsibility for fulfilling this responsibility. Consular officers work closely with foreign ministries and other government institutions. They acquire expertise in local laws, economic conditions, political situations and culture to make informed and rapid decisions affecting U.S. citizens abroad. They help American citizens obtain emergency medical assistance; evacuate American citizens when disasters or armed conflict require; visit arrested Americans and ensure they have access to legal counsel; and screen foreign visa applicants and decide whether to issue or permit them entry into the U.S.

Qualifications:
Applicants for the Foreign Service Written Examination must be between the ages of 20 and 59 and be available for worldwide assignment. Successful applicants must pass the written exam, oral assessment,

background investigation, medical exam, and pre-employment drug screening.

Education:
A bachelor's degree is required for this position. Applicants should be aware that more education increases the likelihood of promotion and advancement.

Preferred/Required Skills:
1.   Effective oral and writing skills
2.   Good interpersonal skills
3.   Good problem solving ability

Training:
Candidates must successfully complete all required agency training.

Grade Level(s): EP-6, Step 5

What to Expect:
1.   Written exam
2.   Oral interviews
3.   Medical screening
4.   Background investigation
5.   Drug testing
6.   Applicant may encounter a waiting period

Salary Range:
The salary for this position depends on education and experience. For example, at the level of a bachelor's degree with no experience, the starting salary is $35,819 per year.

Immigration Agent (Enforcement): Department of Homeland Security, Bureau of Citizenship and Immigration Services

Description:
Enforcement Immigration Agents enforce laws and regulations under the Immigration and Nationality Act. This includes performing a variety of law enforcement and administrative tasks involving employer sanctions, criminal aliens, and the apprehension of absconders from deportation

proceedings. Some of these positions are located in district offices, while others are at Federal Prisons.

Qualifications:
Applicants must be U.S. citizens, possess a valid state driver's license, pass a written test, physical exam, and background investigation. In addition, candidates must have, for three of the last five years immediately before applying for the position (1) resided in the U.S.; or (2) worked in the United States Government as an employee overseas in a federal or military capacity; or (3) been a dependent of a U.S. federal or military employee serving overseas. Applicant must be under 37 years of age. Applicants must have three years of progressively responsible law enforcement experience or possess a bachelor's degree in any field from an accredited college or university, or possess a combination of qualifying education and experience.

Education:
A bachelor's degree or an acceptable combination of education and experience is required for this position. Applicants should be aware that more education increases the likelihood of promotion and advancement.

Preferred/Required Skills:
1. Effective oral and writing skills
2. Good interpersonal skills
3. Good problem solving ability
4. Good judgment
5. Self-control
6. Bilingualism, especially Spanish

Training:
Enforcement Immigration Agents must complete a 14 to 18 week Immigration Officer's Basic Training Course at one of the Service's training centers. They must pass a course of study in immigration law, nationality law, Spanish language, police training, and branch specific operational training.

Grade Level(s): GS-5 through GS-9

What to Expect:
1. Written test

2.   Physical exam
3.   Background investigation
4.   Applicant may encounter a waiting period

Salary Range:
The salary range for this position is $23,000 to $46,000 per year.

Immigration Inspector: Department of Homeland Security, Bureau of Citizenship and Immigration Services

Description:
Immigration Inspectors are the first United States officials that approximately 300 million persons who enter the U.S. will see upon arrival. They can be stationed anywhere that people enter the U.S. from other countries – primarily land ports, seaports, or airports. A key responsibility is to prevent ineligible persons from entering the U.S. Inspectors must be guided in their work by a knowledge of controlling laws, regulations and policies, and court and administrative decisions.

Qualifications:
Applicants must be U.S. citizens, possess a valid state driver's license, and pass a written test, physical exam, and background investigation. In addition, candidates must have, for three of the last five years immediately before applying for the position (1) resided in the U.S.; or (2) worked in the United States Government as an employee overseas in a federal or military capacity; or (3) been a dependent of a U.S. federal or military employee serving overseas. Applicants must be under 37 years of age. Applicants must have three years of progressively responsible law enforcement experience or possess a bachelor's degree in any field from an accredited college or university, or possess a combination of qualifying education and experience.

Education:
A bachelor's degree or an acceptable combination of education and experience is required for this position. Applicants should be aware that more education increases the likelihood of promotion and advancement.

Preferred/Required Skills:
1.   Effective oral and writing skills

2.   Good interpersonal skills
3.   Good problem solving ability
4.   Good judgment
5.   Self-control
6.   Bilingualism, especially Spanish

Training:
Immigration Inspectors will receive a 14 to 18 week Immigration Officer's Basic Training Course at one of the Service's training centers. They must also pass a course of study in immigration law, nationality law, Spanish language, police training, and branch specific operational training.

Grade Level(s): GS-5 through GS-9

What to Expect:
1.   Written test
2.   Physical exam
3.   Background investigation
4.   Applicant may encounter a waiting period

Salary Range:
The salary range for this position is $23,000 to $46,000 per year.

Inspector: Department of the Treasury: Alcohol, Tobacco, and Firearms

Description:
ATF Inspectors conduct inspections, examinations, and investigations. They determine if tax liabilities have been correctly established and paid; determine if transactions requiring payment of excise taxes are reflected in tax returns, etc. ATF Inspectors determine whether operations are in accordance with the laws and regulations. They examine buildings, equipment, finished products, records of firearms and explosives transactions, and conducts interviews with persons connected with regulated industries. They determine if beverage alcohol markets are free of illegal practices; determine whether persons desiring to enter business in the regulated industries meet established legal requirements for obtaining a federal permit or license to conduct operations.

Qualifications:
Applicants must be between 21 and 37 years of age, possess a valid state driver's license, and be U.S. citizens. They must pass an extensive background investigation and pass a medical examination. For the GS-5 level, applicants must possess three years of progressively responsible experience which demonstrates the ability to: (1) Analyze problems to identify significant factors, gather pertinent data, and organize solutions; (2) plan and organize work; and (3) communicate effectively orally and in writing. No test is required. Applicants are evaluated based on experience, formal education, self-development and training within the past five years.

Education:
A minimum high school diploma or General Education Diploma is required for this position. Applicants should be aware that more education may increase the likelihood of promotion and advancement.

Preferred/Required Skills:
1. Effective oral and writing skills
2. Good interpersonal skills
3. Good analytical skills

Training:
Inspectors receive 11 weeks of training at the Federal Law Enforcement Training Center (FLETC) at Glynco, Georgia.

Grade Level(s): GS-5 through GS-7

What to Expect:
1. Background investigation
2. Medical exam

Salary Range:
The salary range for this position is $23,000 to $37,000 per year.

Inspector: Department of the Treasury, U.S. Customs Service

Description:
U.S. Custom Inspectors are responsible for processing persons, baggage, mail and cargo. Inspectors assess and collect Customs duties, taxes, fees,

etc. on imported merchandise. Inspectors also often uncover violations of federal law, such as smuggling, fraud, and theft. Inspectors are stationed at over 300 ports of entry into the U.S. Inspectors assess and interview persons, and detain violators. Inspectors search persons, cargo, vehicles, aircraft and vessels.

Qualifications:
Applicants must be U.S. citizens and pass an extensive background investigation and medical examination. Applicants must possess a bachelor's degree from an accredited college or university or possess three years of generalized experience. Applicants must be willing to accept temporary or permanent assignments in a variety of geographical areas.

Education:
A bachelor's degree and equivalent experience is required for this position. Applicants should be aware that more education increases the likelihood of promotion and advancement.

Preferred/Required Skills:
1.   Good interpersonal skills
2.   Good judgment
3.   Good problem solving ability

Training:
If hired, the applicant must complete all required agency training.

Grade Level(s): GS-1890-05 through GS-1890-07

What to Expect:
1.   Background investigation
2.   Medical exam
3.   Applicant may encounter a waiting period

Salary Range:
The salary range for this position is $25,467 to $41,011 per year at 32 hours per week.

Intelligence Research Specialist: Department of Justice, Federal Bureau of Investigation

Description:
Intelligence Research Specialists conduct extensive research and analysis in the geographical areas handled by the entity to which the position is assigned. They produce intelligence products that are well researched to support studies in geographical or functional areas under investigation or study. They may analyze raw intelligence data to project future events and will prepare presentation materials for briefings and training classes.

Qualifications:
Applicants must be U.S. citizens and consent to a complete background investigation, urinalysis, and polygraph examination. Applicants must provide official transcripts of a bachelor's degree from an accredited college or university. One year of specialized experience equivalent to a GS-9, or three years of progressively higher education leading to a doctoral degree or equivalent is required for GS-11. For GS-12, one year of specialized experience equivalent to a GS-11 is required. The position requires knowledge of a wide range of principles, concepts and research methodologies for analysis of political, social, cultural, physical, geographical, scientific, legal, criminal justice, environmental, and military conditions or trends in foreign or domestic areas.

Education:
This position requires at least a bachelor's degree from an accredited college or university. Applicants should be aware that more education increases the likelihood of promotion and advancement and also may allow the applicant to start at a higher level.

Preferred/Required Skills:
1.   Excellent writing skills
2.   Excellent research and analytical skills
3.   Good problem solving ability
4.   Good judgment in gathering, analyzing, and disseminating intelligence information
5.   Good interpersonal skills

Training:
If hired, the applicant must complete a five week training course at the FBI

Academy in Quantico, Virginia.

Grade Level(s): GS-11 and GS-12

What to Expect:
1. Background investigation
2. Urinalysis
3. Polygraph testing
4. Interviews

Salary Range:
The salary for this position ranges from $46,000 to $73,000, depending on the grade level.

Investigator (Starting Position): Office of Security, Central Intelligence Agency

Description:
It is the function of the CIA to provide timely, reliable, and useful information to the President of the United States and national policy makers. Within this larger mission, it is the role of the Office of Security to provide a comprehensive, world wide security program that protects Agency personnel, programs, information, facilities, and activities. Investigators conduct numerous daily interviews with informants to gather information, which in turn is used by adjudicators. Additional professions within the Office of Security include specialized investigations, risk assessment, polygraph operations, analytical adjudications, physical security, and information systems security.

Qualifications:
Applicant (both self and spouse) must have U.S. citizenship and must successfully complete a thorough screening process to include intellectual and personality screening, a writing test, and interviews. They must also undergo a complete background investigation and medical screening prior to final employment. Applicants must have a college degree with a 3.0/4.0 GPA. All positions require relocation to the Washington D.C. metropolitan area.

Education:
A bachelor's degree is required for this position. Applicants should be aware that more education increases the likelihood of promotion and advancement.

Preferred/Required Skills:
1. Effective oral and writing skills
2. Good interpersonal skills
3. Analytical skills
4. High levels of trustworthiness, integrity, and loyalty to the U.S.

Training:
Security Officers are trained through a system of formal training courses and rotational assignments that provide exposure to a wide variety of security disciplines.

Grade Level(s): Not listed

What to Expect:
1. Employment history check
2. Criminal history check
3. Drug use history check
4. Personal history check
5. Applicant may encounter a waiting period
6. May involve drug testing

Salary Range:
The salary range for this position is $30,000 to $50,000 depending on qualifications, education, and experience.

K-9 Enforcement Officer: Department of the Treasury, U.S. Customs Service

Description:
K-9 Enforcement Officers are responsible for enforcing laws governing the importation of merchandise; interdicting smuggled merchandise and contraband; detecting violations of Customs laws and those of other Federal agencies, i.e.: DEA, Immigration, Agriculture; arresting, if warranted, persons involved in violations. K-9 Enforcement Officers

spend much of their time working directly with their narcotics or explosive/weapons detector dogs and special equipment used in the interdiction of drugs, explosives, weapons, and other substances.

Qualifications:
Applicants must be U.S. citizens and pass an extensive background investigation and medical examination. Applicants must possess a bachelor's degree from an accredited college or university or possess three years of generalized experience.

Education:
A bachelor's degree or equivalent experience is required. Applicants should be aware that more education increases the likelihood of promotion and advancement.

Preferred/Required Skills:
1.   Effective oral and writing skills
2.   Good dog handling skills
3.   Good problem solving ability
4.   Good judgment
5.   Self-control

Training:
K-9 Enforcement Officers attend a ten week dog-handler training course at the U.S. Customs Service Canine Enforcement Training Center located in Front Royal, Virginia.

Grade Level(s): GS-5 through GS-9

What to Expect:
1.   Background investigation
2.   Medical exam
3.   Applicant may encounter a waiting period

Salary Range:
The salary range for this position is $23,000 to $46,000 per year.

Law Enforcement Officer: Department of Transportation, Transportation Security Administration

Description:
As part of the federal government's transition of airport security personnel to federal employees, the TSA seeks to fill Law Enforcement Officer positions at various airports. Duties of the position include monitoring of electronic security surveillance and alarm systems, patrol, surveillance, apprehension of suspects, interviewing of suspects, investigation, and other law enforcement duties.

Qualifications:
Applicants must be U.S. citizens and at least 21, but not over 40 years of age at the time of appointment. One year of specialized experience equivalent to that of the next lower grade or band is required. Applicants must have a valid driver's license; pass drug tests and meet and maintain medical and psychological requirements; maintain eligibility for a secret clearance; carry a firearm and maintain proficiency; and pass training requirements.

Education:
A bachelor's degree or equivalent experience is required. Applicants should be aware that more education may increase the likelihood of promotion and advancement.

Preferred/Required Skills:
1.	Ability to conduct analysis and exercise sound judgment
2.	Knowledge of law enforcement policies, procedures, and regulations,
3.	Good problem solving ability
4.	Skill in visual observation
5.	Ability to be flexible, adaptable, and responsive to needs of the position
6.	Ability to deal effectively with a highly diverse population
7.	Ability to work independently, as well as in teams

Training:
Candidates must successfully complete ten consecutive weeks of training at the Federal Law Enforcement Training Center (FLETC) in Glynco, Georgia.

What to Expect:
1. Background investigation
2. Medical exam
3. Psychological exam
4. Drug testing

Salary Range:
The salary range for this position is $31,000 to $46,000 per year.

Park Ranger (Enforcement): Department of the Interior, National Park Service

Description:
Park Rangers are responsible for the preservation and protection of the National Park Land System. Park Rangers are also responsible for law and regulation enforcement; protection of property; fire control on park land; investigations; apprehension and detention of violators; search and rescue; and the conservation and use of natural resources on national park land.

Qualifications:
This position may be entered from the GS-2 to the GS-5 grade level. An entry level position at the grade of GS-2 requires a high school or General Education Diploma. At the GS-5 level, a four-year degree from an accredited college or university, or two years specialized experience is required. Specialized experience might have been gained in a police force; military police; or by providing protection and law enforcement in places, such as parks, forests, recreational environments, or in performing criminal investigative duties.

Education: A minimum high school diploma or General Education Diploma is required for this position. Applicants should be aware that more education increases the likelihood of promotion and advancement.

Preferred/Required Skills:
1. Good interpersonal skills
2. Effective oral and writing skills
3. Good problem solving ability
4. Good judgment
5. Self-control

Training:
Park Rangers receive approximately 17 to 18 weeks of training. Training is contingent upon National Park Location Assignment.

Grade Level(s): GS-2 to GS-5

What to Expect:
1. Employment history check
2. Criminal history check
3. Drug use history check
4. Personal history check
5. Applicant may encounter a waiting period
6. May involve drug testing

Salary Range:
The salary range for this position is approximately $17,000 to $30,000 per year.

Pilot: Department of the Treasury, U.S. Customs Service

Description:
U.S. Customs Service Pilots are responsible for detecting, sorting, intercepting, tracking, and apprehending smugglers or would-be smugglers. Pilots perform flight duties that involve surveillance of illegal traffic crossing of the borders by air, land, and sea. The Aviation section of U.S. Customs includes the Lockheed P-3AEW, Lockheed P-3, Cessna Citation II, the (CHET) Customs High Endurance Tracker fixed-wing fighter, and the Black Hawk Helicopter.

Qualifications:
Applicants must be U.S. citizens and pass an extensive background investigation and drug test. Applicants must have a current FAA Class I physical examination and possess a current FAA commercial pilot's license.

Education:
A bachelor's degree or equivalent experience is required for this position. Applicants should be aware that more education may increase the likelihood of promotion and advancement.

Preferred/Required Skills:
1. Effective oral and writing skills
2. Commercial pilot skills

Training:
U.S. Customs Service Pilots receive 16 weeks of enforcement training at the Federal Law Enforcement Training Center at Glynco, Georgia.

Grade Level(s): GS-11 through GS-13

What to Expect:
1. Background investigation
2. Drug testing
3. Applicant may encounter a waiting period

Salary Range:
The salary range for this position is $42,000 to $79,000.

Police Officer: Department of the Treasury, Bureau of Printing and Engraving

Description:
Police Officers perform a variety of police tasks. Police Officers perform duties of prevention and detection of crimes by conducting routine patrols of an assigned area or post; submit reports for appropriate action as required; enforce and uphold the integrity of those products produced by the Bureau of Printing and Engraving; preserve the peace of personnel; and respond to assume control of crime scenes or provide medical, fire, or other emergency assistance as directed by authorized authority. They are responsible for apprehending and detaining, with or without warrants, persons accused of committing violations of the law. Police Officers are responsible for control and maintaining order with the countless number of visitors that tour these facilities.

Qualifications:
Applicants must be U.S. citizens, over the age of 21, and pass a background investigation. Applicants must have knowledge of federal, state, and local laws and knowledge of investigative procedures in law enforcement. They must also possess a bachelor's degree from an

accredited college or university, or six months of general experience and six months of specialized experience. Specialized experience may have been gained in a police force, military police, providing protection and law enforcement such as in parks forests, recreational environments, or in performing criminal investigative duties.

Education:
A minimum high school diploma or General Education Diploma is required for this position, depending on experience. Applicants should be aware that more education increases the likelihood of promotion and advancement.

Preferred/Required Skills:
1.   Effective oral and writing skills
2.   Good interpersonal skills
3.   Good problem solving ability
4.   Good judgment
5.   Self-control

Training:
Police Officers will receive an eight week Police Training Course at Glynco, Georgia covering police training and procedures.

Grade Level(s): GS-5 through GS-11

What to Expect:
1.   Background investigation
2.   May encounter a waiting period

Salary Range:
The salary range for this position is $23,000 to $55,000 per year.

Polygraph Examiner: Center for CIA Security, Central Intelligence Agency

Description:
CIA Polygraph Examiners screen and evaluate individuals in an ongoing effort for national security. Most of the positions are located in the Washington, D.C. area, although positions also exist in other major

metropolitan areas. Opportunities for worldwide travel and assignment are available to journeymen examiners.

Qualifications:
U.S. citizenship is required and there are no age limitations. The Center for CIA Security seeks examiners who have graduated from accredited polygraph schools or individuals with sufficient investigative experience who have an interest in the polygraph profession. A baccalaureate from an accredited university or college is mandatory and a GPA of at least 3.0 is desired. All candidates must pass security and medical screenings prior to final acceptance into the CIA. Writing and intellectual examinations and a personality assessment will be administered to all candidates.

Education:
A bachelor's degree is required for this position. Applicants should be aware that more education may increase the likelihood of promotion and advancement.

Preferred/Required Skills:
1.   Good oral communication skills
2.   Ability to write clearly and accurately
3.   Ability to interpret data and formulate conclusions
4.   Knowledge of investigative elements
5.   Strong interpersonal skills
6.   Impeccable personal integrity

Training:
Applicants accepted into the CIA Polygraph Division will be trained and federally certified. The tour of duty in the Polygraph Division is four years with two years dedicated to journeymen level work. All officers will be evaluated in-house prior to being given full-performance certification.

Grade Level(s): Not applicable

What to Expect:
1.   Writing test
2.   Personality assessment
3.   Background investigation
4.   Medical screening
5.   Intellectual screening

6.   Applicant may encounter a waiting period

Salary Range:
The salary for this position is based on experience and expertise.

Refuge Law Enforcement: Department of the Interior, U.S. Fish and Wildlife Service

Description:
Refuge Law Enforcement personnel (1) patrol refuge and refuge complexes for the purpose of enforcing refuge regulations, hunting regulations, and apprehending violators; (2) post and maintain boundary, information, and regulatory signs as needed; and (3) provide information to the public about refuge regulations concerning public use activities, such as beachcombing, hunting, trapping, and fishing. Refuge Law Enforcement personnel also maintain appropriate records and documents pertaining to law enforcement activities, and general maintenance of assigned 4X4 vehicles, ATVs, and personal equipment. Personnel must maintain proficiency with service firearms and may have to appear and provide testimony in court.

Qualifications:
To qualify at the GS-5 grade level, applicants must have one year of specialized experience equivalent to at least the GS-4 grade level in Federal service, or completion of a bachelor's degree from an accredited college or university. Specialized experience is that which is directly related to the position to be filled and which has equipped the candidate with particular knowledge, skills, and abilities to successfully perform the duties of the position.

Education:
A minimum high school diploma or General Education Diploma is required for this position. Applicants should be aware that more education increases the likelihood of promotion and advancement.

Preferred/Required Skills:
1.   Effective oral and writing skills
2.   Good interpersonal skills
3.   Good problem solving ability

4.   Good judgment
5.   Self-control

Training:
Refuge Law Enforcement personnel will attend Basic Law Enforcement for Land Management Agencies and Refuge Officer Basic School at the Federal Law Enforcement Training Center at Glynco, Georgia.

Grade Level(s): GS-5 through GS-9

What to Expect:
1.   Employment history check
2.   Criminal history check
3.   Drug use history check
4.   Personal history check
5.   Applicant may encounter a waiting period
6.   May involve drug testing

Salary Range:
The salary range for this position is $23,000 to $46,000 per year.

Security Protective Officer: Security Protective Service, Central Intelligence Agency

Description:
The mission of the Central Intelligence Agency's Security Protective Service (SPS) is the protection of Agency personnel, facilities, and information through the enforcement of federal laws and agency regulations. This is an entry-level Armed Uniform position located in Northern Virginia.

Qualifications:
Applicants must be U.S. citizens and have a high school diploma or General Education Diploma. They must be at least 21 years old, physically fit, possess a valid driver's license and qualify for a Top Secret security clearance. Applicants must have at least one of the following: military experience (military police or Marine security guard preferred); an associate's or bachelor's degree in criminal justice or a related field; police or significant security experience. Applicants must pass a written

test, then a personal interview. Those selected from the interview will be required to successfully complete a thorough clearance process to include polygraph examinations, medical and psychological screenings, and a background investigation as a condition of employment.

Education:
A minimum high school diploma or General Education Diploma is required for this position. Applicants should be aware that more education increases the likelihood of promotion and advancement.

Preferred/Required Skills:
1.   Effective oral and writing skills
2.   Good interpersonal skills
3.   Good problem solving ability
4.   Good judgment
5.   Self-control

Training:
New appointees receive intensive training at the Federal Law Enforcement Training Center (FLETC) in Glynco, Georgia, and specialized instruction at SPS training facilities. Training includes course work in police procedures, psychology, police-community relations, criminal law, first aid, laws of arrest, search and seizure, and physical defense techniques.

Grade Level(s): Not listed

What to Expect:
1.   Written test
2.   Interview
3.   Background investigation
4.   Medical screening
5.   Psychological screening
6.   Polygraph test
7.   Applicant may encounter a waiting period

Salary Range: Not listed

Special Agent: Department of Justice, Drug Enforcement Administration

Description:
DEA Special Agents investigate violations of federal law dealing with controlled substances, illegal narcotics, and drug abuse. DEA Special Agents enforce controlled substances laws and regulations, and focus on organizations and/or individuals involved with growing, manufacturing, and distributing controlled substances and/or illegal narcotics, within or destined for the United States. The DEA is responsible for interdicting illegal drug traffic before reaching the user. DEA Special Agents may be involved with specific units with focus on Laboratory Services, Aviation, or Special Operations (Task Forces), and others. Special Agents may be called upon to do surveillance and/or undercover work.

Qualifications:
Applicants must be U.S. citizens, be between the ages of 21 and 35, and possess a valid state driver's license. They must be available for relocation. Applicants must possess one year of law enforcement experience; however, some education may be substituted. Applicants must also pass a physical exam.

Education:
A minimum high school diploma or General Education Diploma is required for this position. Applicants should be aware that more education increases the likelihood of promotion and advancement.

Preferred/Required Skills:
1. Effective oral and writing skills
2. Good interpersonal skills
3. Good problem solving ability
4. Good judgment
5. Self-control
6. Bilingualism, especially Spanish and Middle Eastern languages, is a plus
7. Sound mental and physical health

Training:
DEA Special Agents will attend a fourteen week training academy at the FBI Academy in Quantico, Virginia.

Grade Level(s): GS-9 to GS-12

What to Expect:
1. Employment history check
2. Criminal history check
3. Drug use history check
4. Personal history check
5. Physical exam
6. May involve drug testing
7. Applicant may encounter a waiting period

Salary Range: The salary range for this position is $35,000 to $66,000 per year.

Special Agent: Department of Justice, Federal Bureau of Investigation

Description:
FBI Special Agents investigate violations of federal law except for those already designated to another federal agency. FBI Special Agents have jurisdiction on over 260 violations. Special Agents may be involved with specific units with focus on Foreign Counterintelligence, Organized Crime, Domestic or International Terrorism, White Collar Crime, Governmental Fraud, Public Corruption, Financial Crimes, Civil Rights Programs, Laboratory Services, Fingerprint Identification, National Crime Information Center, and others. Special Agents may be called upon to do surveillance and/or undercover work.

Qualifications:
The applicant must be a U.S. citizen, possess a valid state driver's license, and must be between the ages of 23 and 37. Applicants must successfully complete a written test and interview, which will be followed by a thorough background investigation. Applicants must pass a physical exam, meet vision and hearing requirements, and be available for relocation. The five entrance programs under which Special Agents qualify are Accounting, Diversified, Engineering/Science, Language, and Law. Applicants accepted must serve a two year probationary period.

Education:
A bachelor's degree is required for this position. Applicants should be aware that more education increases the likelihood of promotion and advancement.

Skills: Critical skills currently needed are:
1.   Computer Science and other Information Technology specialties
2.   Engineering
3.   Physical Sciences (Physics, Chemistry, Biology, etc.)
4.   Foreign Language Proficiency (Arabic, Chinese, Farsi, Pashto, Urdu, Japanese, Korean, Russian, and Vietnamese)
5.   Foreign Counterintelligence
6.   Counterterrorism
7.   Military Intelligence experience

Training:
FBI Special Agents will attend a 16 week training academy at Quantico, Virginia. Special Agents may also receive more specialized training after the FBI Academy, depending on the area to which the Agent is going to be assigned.

Grade Level(s): GS-10 to GS-13

What to Expect:
1.   Written tests
2.   Interview
3.   Background investigation
4.   Vision testing
5.   Hearing testing

Salary Range:
The salary during Academy Training (GS-10) is $43,000 per year. After training, the salary depends on the grade and ranges from $53,000 to $58,000.

Special Agent (Deputy Marshals): Department of Justice, U.S. Marshals Service

Description:
U.S. Deputy Marshals are responsible for enforcing federal laws that were directed for federal interests on the local level. U.S. Deputy Marshals act as the enforcement agents for the Executive Branch of government. U.S. Deputy Marshals may be assigned to different units with varying missions, such as: Court Security; Federal Fugitives; Prisoner Custody; Prisoner Transport; Prisoner Airline; Witness Protection; National Asset Seizure and Forfeiture; Execution of Court Orders; Air Operations Branch; the Missile Escort Program; and Special Operations. Special Operations responds to emergency situations, such as civil disturbances, terrorist events, hostage situations, etc. U.S. Deputy Marshals may be called upon to do surveillance and/or undercover work.

Qualifications:
Applicants must be U.S. citizens, be between 21 and 35 years of age, possess a valid driver's license, and pass an extensive background investigation, physical test, and a medical examination. Applicants must possess a bachelor's degree in any field from an accredited college or university or three years of general experience may be substituted for education.

Education:
A bachelor's degree is required for this position. Applicants should be aware that more education increases the likelihood of promotion and advancement.

Preferred/Required Skills:
1. Effective oral and writing skills
2. Good interpersonal skills
3. Good problem solving ability
4. Good judgment
5. Self-control

Training:
U.S. Deputy Marshals receive 14 weeks of training. The first eight weeks consists of the Basic Criminal Investigators Course at the Federal Law Enforcement Training Center, Glynco, Georgia. The next six weeks

consists of the Basic U.S. Deputy Marshal Training School, also at Glynco, Georgia.

Grade Level(s): GS-5 through GS-7

What to Expect:
1.   Background investigation
2.   Physical test
3.   Medical exam
4.   Applicant may encounter a waiting period

Salary Range:
The salary range for this position is $23,000 to $40,000 per year.

Special Agent: Department of the Treasury: Alcohol, Tobacco, and Firearms

Description:
ATF Special Agents investigate violations of Federal Explosive Laws. ATF Special Agents enforce federal law and regulations, and focus on organizations and/or individuals involved with illegal trafficking, illegal possession and criminal use of firearms; illegal manufacturing and distributing of alcohol; illicit non-paid tax on cigarettes and/or alcohol. The ATF is responsible for the interdiction of illegal firearms and illegal explosives. ATF Special Agents may be involved with specific units that focus on National Response Teams; The Arson Task Force; Federal Firearms Laws; Drug Enforcement Efforts; Jamaican Organized Crime; Outlaw Motorcycle Gangs; Street Gangs; White Supremacist Groups; Firearms Tracing Center; National Laboratory Center; National Explosive Tracing Center; etc. Special Agents may be called upon to do surveillance and/or undercover work.

Qualifications:
Applicants must be U.S. citizens, be between 21 and 37 years of age, and possess a valid state driver's license. In addition, they must pass an extensive background investigation, a rigorous physical fitness test and medical examination. Applicants must possess a bachelor's degree in any field from an accredited college or university, or three years of general experience may be substituted for education.

Preferred/Required Skills:
1. Effective oral and writing skills
2. Good interpersonal skills
3. Good problem solving ability
4. Good judgment
5. Self-control

Training:
Special Agents receive formal training and on-the-job training. Special Agents will receive an eight week Criminal Investigators Training Course at the Federal Law Enforcement Training Center at Glynco, Georgia. Upon completion of the Criminal Investigators Training Course, agents receive New Agent Training where they will receive highly specialized training in their duties as ATF Agents.

Grade Level(s): GS-5 through GS-7

What to Expect:
1. Background investigation
2. Physical fitness testing
3. Medical exam
4. Applicant may encounter a waiting period

Salary Range:
The salary range for this position is $23,000 to $37,000 per year.

Special Agent: Department of the Treasury, Internal Revenue Service

Description:
Special Agents conduct investigations of suspected offenders of tax law. The tax money collected is used to support Federal Programs. Special Agents are involved with investigations, criminal and civil, dealing with Internal Revenue laws, generally involving tax fraud or evasion. Special Agents may be involved with various units within the IRS, such as: Strike Force, Drug Task Forces and Intelligence. Special Agents investigate a wide variety of crimes such as illegal tax protesters, money laundering, and banking violations.

Qualifications:
Applicants must be U.S. citizens, be between 21 and 37 years of age, and possess a valid state driver's license. In addition, they must pass an extensive background investigation and medical examination. Applicants must possess a bachelor's degree, with at least 24 semester hours of accounting and related business or law courses. Applicants who possess a bachelor's degree in business or law must have at least 15 semester hours in accounting. Applicants may also have three years of accounting or related business experience in order to qualify for this position.

Education:
A bachelor's degree is required for this position. Applicants should be aware that more education increases the likelihood of promotion and advancement.

Preferred/Required Skills:
1.   Effective oral and writing skills
2.   Good interpersonal skills
3.   Good problem solving ability
4.   Good investigative skills

Training:
IRS Special Agents will receive a total of 21 weeks of training. Training consists of the Basic Criminal Investigator Course at the Federal Law Enforcement Training Center at Glynco, Georgia; on-the-job training; an Introductory Special Agent course; Tax Law for Criminal Investigators; and Special Agent Investigative Techniques.

Grade Level(s): GS-5 through GS-12

What to Expect:
1.   Background investigation
2.   Medical exam

Salary Range:
The salary range for this position is $23,000 to $66,000 per year.

Special Agent: Department of the Treasury, Secret Service

Description:
Special Agents in the Secret Service have two missions: protection and investigations. Special Agents are responsible for protecting the President, Vice President, President-elect, Vice President-elect; visiting heads of foreign states or governments and their spouses; other distinguished foreign visitors; major presidential and vice presidential candidates and their spouses within 120 days before the election; and former Presidents and their spouses. Special Agents also investigate violations of laws involving U.S. currency (i.e.: counterfeiting). Agents are involved with the investigations of counterfeiting of certain government identification, devices, theft, and forgery of U.S. government checks and bonds. Special Agents also are responsible for investigations dealing with credit card fraud and computer fraud (ATM machines, computer chips in car phones, PIN numbers).

Qualifications:
Applicants must be U.S. citizens, less than 35 years of age, and have knowledge of federal, state, and local laws. They must also have knowledge of investigative procedures in law enforcement. Applicants must pass an extensive background investigation, as well as a comprehensive medical examination. Applicants must possess a bachelor's degree from an accredited college or university, or in some cases applicants will be considered with three years of experience (in which two of the years are performing criminal investigation).

Education:
A bachelor's degree is required for this position. Applicants should be aware that more education increases the likelihood of promotion and advancement.

Preferred/Required Skills:
1. Effective oral and writing skills
2. Good interpersonal skills
3. Good problem solving ability
4. Good judgment
5. Self-control

Training:
Special Agents receive 11 weeks of training at the Federal Law Enforcement Training Center at Glynco, Georgia. Upon successful completion of this course, agents move on to 11 weeks of training in Laurel, Maryland. Agents are then required to perform formal O-T-J (on the job training) for approximately one year.

Grade Level(s): GS-5 through GS-12

What to Expect:
1. Background investigation
2. Medical exam
3. Applicant may encounter a waiting period

Salary Range:
The salary range for this position is $28,000 to $66,000 per year.

Special Agent: Department of the Treasury, U.S. Customs Service

Description:
Special Agents are involved with planning and conducting investigations relating to alleged and/or suspected violations of the U.S. Customs law (i.e., illegal contraband, currency that supports criminal activity, intercepting illegal high-technology exports, preventing fraud). Special Agents perform searches and seizures and make arrests. Special Agents may also be assigned to various units within the U.S. Customs Services, such as the Currency/Money Laundering Program, Pornography Enforcement, or Export Enforcement. Special Agents may be called upon to do surveillance and/or undercover work.

Qualifications:
Applicants must be U.S. citizens, be between 21 and 35 years of age, and must possess a valid state driver's license. Applicants must pass an extensive background investigation and a medical examination. Applicants must possess a bachelor's degree from an accredited college or university or possess one year of general experience and two years of specialized experience. Applicants must also be willing to travel and work overtime.

Education:
A bachelor's degree or equivalent experience is required for this position. Applicants should be aware that more education increases the likelihood of promotion and advancement.

Preferred/Required Skills:
1. Effective oral and writing skills
2. Good interpersonal skills
3. Good problem solving ability
4. Good judgment
5. Self-control

Training:
Special Agents must complete a 14 week training course at the Federal Law Enforcement Training Center at Glynco, Georgia. Training includes such areas as child pornography, fraud, smuggling, surveillance techniques and export investigations.

Grade Level(s): GS-5 through GS-12

What to Expect:
1. Background investigation
2. Medical exam
3. Applicant may encounter a waiting period

Salary Range:
The salary range for this position is $23,000 to $66,000 per year.

Supervisory Investigator, Area Director: Department of the Treasury, U.S. Customs Service

Description:
This position is located in the Operations Division within the U.S. Customs Service (USCS) and Office of International Affairs. The primary purpose of this position is to direct operations and support functions of the Customs Attache offices for which he or she is responsible. The Director provides technical advice and supervision to Customs Attaches, Senior Customs Representatives and subordinate staff, most of whom are Criminal Investigators assigned to offices within his or her assigned

geographic area. The Director responds and resolves technical and operational questions regarding the Foreign Operations investigative programs and performs other duties as assigned.

Qualifications:
Applications are accepted from Department of Treasury and U.S. Customs Service status candidates only. Applicants must have one year of specialized experience typically in or related to the investigation of criminal violations that provided the specific knowledge, skills, and abilities to perform successfully the duties of the position. The one year of qualifying specialized experience must have been equivalent to the level of difficulty and responsibility comparable to the next lower grade in the Federal service. Applicants must also demonstrate the ability to manage and direct major international investigative operations or programs. Applicants must pass a background investigation and may be required, if hired, to maintain a level of fitness and undergo regular physical examinations. The position requires the ability to qualify in the use of firearms after appointment and may require the carrying and use of firearms in the performance of the duties of the position.

Education:
A graduate degree or acceptable level of experience is required for this position.

Preferred/Required Skills:
1.   Effective oral and writing skills
2.   Good interpersonal skills
3.   Good analytical skills
4.   Ability to interact with senior level officials internal and external to Customs
5.   Ability to identify key issues and develop recommendations that significantly modify and improve a major program
6.   Ability to supervise, plan, direct, and review work of subordinates
7.   Ability to implement EEO principles and practices, including Special Emphasis Programs

Training:
No specific agency/state training noted.

Grade Level(s): GS-1811-15/15 with promotion potential to GS-15

What to Expect:
1. Background investigation
2. Physical exam
3. Fitness exam

Salary Range:
The salary range for this position is $92,000 to $119,000 per year.

Supervisory Law Enforcement Officer

Description:
The incumbent holds the rank of Sergeant as a first level supervisory Law Enforcement Officer, responsible for directing the work of subordinate officers, and assisting in and performing the administration of complex law enforcement duties primarily concerned with alleged or suspected offenses against the security of our national airports and criminal laws. Duties include the full range of law enforcement tasks. Supervisory duties include assigning tasks; determining priorities; monitoring and evaluating performance; coaching and developing employees; and other duties appropriate to the position.

Qualifications:
Applicants must be U.S. citizens and at least 21 years of age at the time of appointment. One year of specialized experience equivalent to that of the next lower grade or band is required. Applicants must pass drug tests and meet and maintain medical and psychological requirements; maintain eligibility for a secret clearance; carry a firearm and maintain proficiency; pass training requirements; and have a valid driver's license.

Education:
A bachelor's degree or equivalent experience is required for this position. Applicants should be aware that more education increases the likelihood of promotion and advancement.

Preferred/Required Skills:
1. Ability to conduct analysis and exercise sound judgment
2. Knowledge of law enforcement regulations, policies, and procedures
3. Good problem solving ability
4. Skill in visual observation

5.   Ability to be highly flexible, adaptable, and responsive to the needs of the position
6.   Ability to deal effectively with a highly diverse population
7.   Ability to manage a diverse workforce and lead others

Training:
Candidates must successfully complete ten consecutive weeks of training at the Federal Law Enforcement Training Center (FLETC) in Glynco, Georgia.

Grade Level(s): SV-1801-H

What to Expect:
1.   Background investigation
2.   Medical exam
3.   Psychological exam
4.   Drug testing

Salary Range:
The salary range for this position is $44,000 to $68,000 per year, plus locality pay where applicable.

Uniformed Police Officer: Department of the Treasury, Secret Service

Description:
The Uniformed Division is divided into three branches: Administration and Support; Foreign Mission; and the White House. Police Officers perform a variety of police tasks, but maintain one mission, which is protection. The primary focus of the Uniformed Division is the protection of the President and his immediate family while residing at the White House. Secondly, the Uniformed Division provides protection for the official residence of the Vice President and his immediate family, foreign diplomatic missions in the Washington, D.C. area, and buildings with Presidential offices. Uniformed Police Officers perform routine patrols of an assigned area or post, vehicular patrols, and foot patrols. The Uniformed Division also provides support to the overall Secret Service, by use of K-9 units, countersniper teams, etc.

Qualifications:
Applicants must be U.S. citizens, less than 35 years of age, and possess a valid driver's license. Applicants must pass a written exam, comprehensive examination, and a background investigation. Applicants must also possess a high school diploma or General Education Diploma.

Education:
A minimum high school diploma or General Education Diploma is required for this position. Applicants should be aware that more education increases the likelihood of promotion and advancement.

Preferred/Required Skills:
1. Effective oral and writing skills
2. Good interpersonal skills
3. Good problem solving ability
4. Good judgment
5. Self-control

Training:
Uniformed Police Officers will attend an eight week Police Training Course in Glynco, Georgia covering police training and procedures, followed by seven weeks of training at the Secret Service training facilities in Washington, D.C.

Grade Level(s): Not Available

What to Expect:
1. Written exam
2. Comprehensive exam
3. Background investigation
4. Applicant may encounter a waiting period

Salary Range:
The starting salary for this position is $39,025 per year.

U.S. Park Police (National Capitol Region): Department of the Interior, National Parks Service

Description:
U.S. Park Police perform law enforcement duties in the Capitol area.

Qualifications:
Applicants must be over the age of 21, but not yet 35 years of age, possess U.S. citizenship, and have completed two years of study at an accredited college or university. They must also have two years of responsible experience, or an acceptable combination of experience and education. Applicants must pass a background investigation, oral, written, and physical examinations.

Education:
A minimum high school diploma or General Education Diploma is required for this position. Applicants should be aware that more education may increase the likelihood of promotion and advancement.

Preferred/Required Skills:
1. Good interpersonal skills
2. Effective writing skills
3. Good problem solving ability
4. Good judgment
5. Self-control

Training:
If hired, the applicant must successfully complete all required agency training.

Grade Level(s): Not Available

What to Expect:
1. Background investigation
2. Oral exam
3. Written exam
4. Physical exam
5. Applicant may encounter a waiting period
6. May involve drug testing

Salary Range: Not listed

Victims Specialist: Department of Justice, Federal Bureau of Investigation

Description:
At the GS-9 level, Victim Specialists have direct contact with the victims of crime to ensure they receive full access to rights and services available through the federal justice system, as provided under the FBI's Victim-Witness Assistance Program (VWAP). They make presentations outside the agency on victims' issues; conduct research; respond to crime scenes; provide training to other agencies; and monitor and assess the VWAP within the field office.

Qualifications:
Applicants must be U.S. citizens and consent to a complete background investigation, urinalysis, and polygraph examination. All applicants must have one year of specialized experience equivalent to at least the next lower grade level. They must have knowledge of victimology and victim assistance issues and resources, as well as policies and procedures connected with the federal Victim-Witness Assistance Programs, in addition to knowledge of the criminal justice system, including the roles of investigators, prosecutors, the judiciary, and corrections. Victim Specialists must be able to establish and maintain effective working relationships with FBI agents and/or other law enforcement personnel; attorneys; and/or representatives from federal, state, and local agencies and service organizations. At the GS-11 level, applicants must have the ability to analyze programs and then develop and implement improvements. Applicants must provide transcripts and a resume.

Education:
For the grade of GS-9, a master's degree or the equivalent is required. For GS-11, three full years of progressively higher level graduate education leading to a Ph.D., or a Ph.D., is required.

Preferred/Required Skills:
1. Effective oral and writing skills
2. Good interpersonal skills
3. Research skills

Training:
No specific agency/state training noted.

Grade Level(s): GS-9 through GS-11

What to Expect:
1.   Interview
2.   Background investigation
3.   Drug testing
4.   Polygraph testing

Salary Range:
The salary range for GS-9 is $40,000 to $52,000 per year. The range for GS-11 is $48,000 to $62,000 per year.

Wildlife Special Agent: Department of the Interior, U.S. Fish and Wildlife Service

Description:
Wildlife Special Agents are involved with the planning and conducting of investigations relating to alleged and/or suspected violations of Federal Law involving the protection and conservation of wildlife. Criminal Investigators may be called upon to do surveillance and/or undercover work, participate in raids, interview witnesses, question suspects, and make arrests.

Qualifications:
Applicants must be U.S. citizens, over the age of 21 but have not yet reached 37 years of age, pass a background investigation, and pass a physical examination. Pre-employment medical exams are at the expense of the individual who is applying. Applicants must possess a four year degree at an accredited college or university, or possess three years of general experience.

Education:
A minimum high school diploma or General Education Diploma is required for this position. Applicants should be aware that more education increases the likelihood of promotion and advancement.

Preferred/Required Skills:
1. Effective oral and writing skills
2. Good interpersonal skills
3. Good problem solving ability
4. Good judgment
5. Self-control

Training:
Wildlife Special Agents attend a 14 week training course at Glynco, Georgia. Upon completion of the training school, Agents will receive additional on-the-job training in one of seven different designated law enforcement districts.

Grade Level(s): GS-5 through GS-9

What to Expect:
1. Employment history check
2. Criminal history check
3. Drug use history check
4. Personal history check
5. Applicant may encounter a waiting period

Salary Range:
The salary range for this position is approximately $23,000 to $30,000 per year.

FEDERAL POSITIONS REQUIRING A MASTER'S DEGREE

Intelligence Research Specialist: Department of the Treasury: U.S. Customs Service, Office of Intelligence of the Financial Crimes Enforcement Network

Description:
The OOI serves as a center for facilitating the development and coordination of financial intelligence information for use within the intelligence and law enforcement communities in order to detect, deter, and investigate money laundering activities. Intelligence Research Specialists conduct analyses of money laundering associated with organized crime, counterterrorism and counternarcotics activities. They

utilize their expertise to detect important trends that could affect national security, make reports of their analyses, conduct liaisons with national level representatives of intelligence and law enforcement agencies, and represent FinCEN in meetings and conferences.

Qualifications:
Applicants must have one year of specialized experience equivalent to the next lower grade level. For GS-09, two full years of progressively higher level graduate education, or a master's or equivalent graduate degree may substitute for experience. Applicants must pass drug screening and an intensive background investigation.

Education:
A master's or equivalent graduate degree is required for this position. More education increases the likelihood of promotion and advancement.

Preferred/Required Skills:
1.   Effective oral and writing skills
2.   Expertise in conducting research and analysis of complex technical issues
3.   Ability to develop formal reports, analyses, correspondence and summaries
4.   Good interpersonal skills

Training:
No specific agency training noted.

Grade Level(s): GS-9 with GS-13 promotion potential

What to Expect:
1.   Background investigation
2.   Drug testing

Salary Range:
The salary range for this position is $38,000 to $86,000 per year.

PART THREE
Research Positions

POSITIONS REQUIRING A BACHELOR'S DEGREE

Community Coordinator: Vera Institute of Justice

Description:
The Community Coordinator coordinates the segment of a corrections program that brings community-based service providers into the correctional facility to meet with project participants and introduce their services. The Community Coordinator recruits and maintains an extensive network of service providers across New York City; schedules and coordinates trips to the facility; spends time with individual participants matching them with services; and assists in facilitating groups of participants in other subject areas of the project.

Qualifications:
A bachelor's degree and excellent interpersonal and organizational skills are required for the position. Previous experience in criminal justice, community network building, and group facilitation is a plus, as is bilingualism in Spanish. Applicants and employees must meet the New York State Department of Correctional Services' requirements for working inside a correctional facility.

Education:
A bachelor's degree is required for this position. Applicants should be aware that more education increases the likelihood of promotion and advancement.

Preferred/Required Skills:
1.   Excellent interpersonal skills
2.   Excellent organizational skills
3.   Bilingualism in Spanish is a plus

Training:
No specific agency/state training noted.

Grade Level(s): Not applicable

What to Expect:
1.   Interview

Salary Range:
The salary range for this position is approximately $28,000 to $35,000 per year.

Intake Interviewer: Vera Institute of Justice

Description:
The Intake Interviewer for Vera's Adolescent Portable Therapy (APT) is responsible for conducting interviews with adolescents and parents, performing structured observations, data management, assisting in the preparation of reports, and facilitating relations with program and corrections staff. Travel to neighborhoods in New York City using public transportation is required, as well as periodic site visits to incarcerated youth in upstate New York State facilities.

Qualifications:
A bachelor's degree is required for this position, as well as fluency in Spanish. Preference will be given to candidates with experience working with adolescents or incarcerated populations; knowledge of, and experience in social science research; field research experience; and cross cultural experience.

Education:
A bachelor's degree is required for this position. Applicants should be aware that more education increases the likelihood of promotion and advancement.

Preferred/Required Skills:
1.   Effective oral and writing skills
2.   Excellent interpersonal skills
3.   Strong organizational skills
4.   Ability to speak Spanish fluently

Training:
No specific agency training noted.

Grade Level(s): Not applicable

What to Expect:
1. Interview

Salary Range:
The salary range for this position is commensurate with experience.

Investigator I: Habeas Corpus Resource Center

Description:
The HCRC Investigator I assists in planning, organizing and conducting investigations related to the representation of death row inmates in habeas corpus proceedings. Some typical duties include: locating, retrieving, reviewing, and analyzing factual materials and records; identifying, locating and interviewing family members, law enforcement officials, witnesses, and other persons; conferring with attorneys on potential legal issues; drafting reports, summaries and witness statements; and maintaining filing and information reference systems.

Qualifications:
Applicants must have the equivalent of a bachelor's degree, preferably with a major in criminal justice, law, psychology, sociology, or journalism and two years experience in general investigation or one year of experience in capital investigations, or one year as a Litigation Support Assistant with HCRC.

Education:
A bachelor's degree is required for this position. Applicants should be aware that more education increases the likelihood of promotion and advancement.

Preferred/Required Skills:
1. Investigative skills
2. Research skills
3. Organizational skills

Training:
No specific agency/state training noted.

Grade Level(s): HCRC Investigator I

What to Expect:
1.   Interview

Salary Range:
The salary range for this position is $47,000 to $57,000 per year.

Investigator II: Habeas Corpus Resource Center

Description:
The HCRC Investigator II conducts complex investigations on capital cases and exercises a high degree of initiative and independent judgment to independently perform the full range of investigatory duties under general supervision. They may be required to work holidays, evening and weekend hours, and must travel as necessary.

Qualifications:
Applicants must have the equivalent of a bachelor's degree, preferably with a major in criminal justice, law, psychology, sociology, or journalism and two years of experience in capital investigations, or two years as a Habeas Corpus Investigator I. Additional college education may be substituted for a portion of the required experience.

Education:
A bachelor's degree is required for this position. Applicants should be aware that more education increases the likelihood of promotion and advancement.

Preferred/Required Skills:
1.   Investigative skills
2.   Research skills
3.   Organizational skills

Training:
No specific agency training noted.

Grade Level(s): HCRC Investigator II

What to Expect:
1.   Interview

Salary Range:
The salary range for this position is $48,000 to $62,000 per year.

Program Coordinator: Vera Institute of Justice, National Associates Program on Youth Justice

Description:
The Program Coordinator provides assistance to state and county officials who are engaged in reforms related to juvenile justice and child welfare issues. The YJP does this by offering peer-to-peer assistance and research support. The Program Coordinator requests information; maintains the program's web site; performs administrative functions; produces the program newsletter; and plans, coordinates, and organizes meetings and events in New York City and elsewhere.

Qualifications:
Applicants must have a bachelor's degree and a demonstrated interest in and understanding of criminal justice, juvenile justice, and child welfare policies. Experience with word processing, Microsoft Excel, Power Point, Publisher, and Front Page is required. Previous administrative experience is desirable.

Education:
A bachelor's degree is required for this position. Applicants should be aware that more education increases the likelihood of promotion and advancement.

Preferred/Required Skills:
1. Excellent oral and writing skills
2. Good interpersonal skills
3. Excellent organizational skills
4. Computer skills

Training:
No specific agency/state training noted.

Grade Level(s): Not applicable

What to Expect:
1.   Interview

Salary Range:
The salary range for this position is approximately $28,000 to $33,000 per year.

Program Officer: The Ford Foundation, Peace and Social Justice Program

Description:
The Program Officer will develop a portfolio of grants and manage other activities devoted to building effective justice systems that promote fairness, respect for rights, and the rule of law with an emphasis on criminal justice. The Program Officer will review existing lines of work; formulate grant-making strategies and initiatives; solicit, review and respond to grant proposals; monitor existing grants and other developments in the field; and prepare recommendations for Foundation funding.

Qualifications:
The position requires significant experience in the area of criminal justice from a human or civil rights perspective; familiarity with relevant programs and institutions in the U.S. and, ideally, other regions of the world; demonstrated analytical, organizational, and oral and written communications skills; and the ability to work closely with colleagues and grantees of diverse backgrounds and perspectives. Also desirable are: advanced training in law, criminology, or another relevant field; fluency in a second language; and familiarity with philanthropy and nonprofit sector issues. Applicants must supply cover letter, resume, and a brief writing sample.

Education:
A minimum bachelor's degree is required, but a graduate degree is desirable. Applicants should be aware that more education increases the likelihood of promotion and advancement.

Preferred/Required Skills:
1.   Oral and written communications skills

2.   Analytical skills
3.   Organizational skills
4.   Interpersonal skills

Training:
No specific agency/state training noted.

Grade Level(s): Not applicable

What to Expect:
1.   Interview

Salary Range: Based on education and experience.

Project Director: Police Executive Research Forum (PERF)

Description:
The in-house project director will supervise all aspects of PERF's Jamaica initiative to reduce crime in Kingston, Jamaica through the establishment of a community policing program. The position involves writing, training coordination, and oral communication at a high level to represent PERF with federal funders and police and criminal justice officials both in the U.S. and Jamaica. The director will manage federal grants and develop proposals, as well as work with police agencies.

Qualifications:
Experience in international policing, community and problem solving policing, writing grants and developing proposals is required. An undergraduate degree is required, with a master's degree preferred.

Education:
A minimum bachelor's degree is required for this position. Applicants should be aware that more education increases the likelihood of promotion and advancement.

Preferred/Required Skills:
1.   Leadership and administrative skills
2.   Excellent interpersonal skills
3.   Excellent oral and writing skills

4.   Excellent problem solving skills

Training:
No specific agency training noted.

Grade Level(s): Not applicable

What to Expect:
1.   Interview

Salary Range:
The salary range for this position is commensurate with experience and education.

Research Analyst: Judicial Council of California

Description:
This is a senior research position in the Administrative Office of the Courts (AOC) with the position assigned to the Center for Families, Children, and the Courts. Duties include needs assessment and project design; data collection and training; development of analysis plans; project presentation and implementation; press releases; and reports. The position is located in San Francisco.

Qualifications:
Applicants must have the equivalent of a bachelor's degree, preferably with major course work in statistics, math, social science, or public/business administration with a concentration in research methods. They must also have at least three years of work experience.

Education:
A bachelor's degree is required for this position. Applicants should be aware that more education increases the likelihood of promotion and advancement.

Preferred/Required Skills:
1.   Good oral and writing skills
2.   Good research skills
3.   Good organizational skills

Training:
No specific agency training noted.

Grade Level(s): Not applicable

What to Expect:
1.   Interview

Salary Range:
The salary range for this position is $60,000 to $70,000 per year.

Research Intern: Vera Institute of Justice

Description:
Interns assist with research, development, and evaluation within the juvenile justice field. They play a role in researching juvenile justice reform in other jurisdictions and help gather and generate information to inform the development of current juvenile justice projects. Responsibilities include literature reviews and Internet searches, data analysis, conducting interviews, data entry and cleanup, and other project-related assistance.

Qualifications:
Ideal candidates are hard-working, detail-oriented, able to follow instructions, and able to work well, both as part of a team and independently. Because the intern deals with sensitive and confidential information, he or she is required to sign a strict confidentiality agreement. Knowledge of, and experience in social science research, especially in the areas of criminology or criminal justice, is a plus. Knowledge of SPSS is preferred, but not required. Applicants must submit a resume of education and experience.

Education:
A bachelor's degree is preferred for this position.

Preferred/Required Skills:
1.   Effective oral and writing skills
2.   Research skills
3.   Good problem solving ability

4.   Good interpersonal skills

Training:
No specific agency/state training noted.

Grade Level(s): Not applicable

What to Expect:
1.   Interview

Salary Range:
This is not a salaried position. The position pays $10 per hour.

POSITIONS REQUIRING A MASTER'S DEGREE

International Center Director: National Institute of Justice

Description:
The Center coordinates the international research, development and dissemination activities of the NIJ. It also serves as a point of contact for a growing number of international colleagues, as well as the federal research and policy offices with which NIJ has partnerships. The Center has developed a series of research projects on human trafficking and the impact of transnational crime on various sectors in the U.S.

Qualifications:
Applicants must be U.S. citizens, have significant international experience, be conversant in criminal justice research and developmental methodology, be entrepreneurial in spirit, and possess first class managerial capabilities. Knowledge of international legal issues would be helpful for this position.

Education:
Most applicants for this position will have an advanced degree.

Preferred/Required Skills:
1.   Superior managerial skills
2.   Excellent interpersonal skills

Training:
No specific agency training noted.

Grade Level(s): Not applicable

What to Expect:
1.   Interview

Salary Range:
The salary range for this position is commensurate with experience and education.

Project Director: Vera Institute of Justice

Description:
The Project Director leads a demonstration project that tests a new model of respite care for ungovernable or truant youth in the city's PINS (Persons in Need of Supervision) system. The Project Director is responsible for monitoring the results and changing the model to reflect lessons learned from early experience; negotiates the precise division of responsibilities between Vera and the provider; and manages the relationship so the program serves the interests of each organization and the PINS families. The project director will supervise a respite staff of about twenty persons, oversee the budget, and speak publicly regarding the project.

Qualifications:
Applicants must have a master's degree or Ph.D. The position requires experience working with adolescents, families, and governmental agencies. Applicants must be willing to work long hours, including during the night and on weekends. Applicants should supply a curriculum vitae.

Education:
A master's degree or Ph.D. is required for this position.

Preferred/Required Skills:
1.   Strong management skills
2.   Strong writing skills
3.   Strong public speaking skills

Training:
No specific agency training noted.

Grade Level(s): Not applicable

What to Expect:
1.   Interview

Salary Range:
The top salary for this position $85,000 per year.

Research Associate: Vera Institute of Justice

Description:
Research Associates carry out research, development, and evaluation of work within the juvenile justice field. They are responsible for managing and analyzing complex computerized databases and interpreting statistical data, as well as conducting interviews and writing reports.

Qualifications:
Applicants must have a master's degree in criminal justice or a related discipline; significant experience and skill in managing databases and conducting statistical analyses using SPSS or other statistical software; and experience working in applied research settings, especially in the criminal justice field. Applicants should supply a curriculum vitae.

Education:
A master's degree is required for this position.

Preferred/Required Skills:
1.   Excellent writing and communication skills
2.   Excellent research skills

Training:
No specific agency training noted.

Grade Level(s): Not applicable
What to Expect:
1.   Interview

Salary Range:
The salary range for this position is commensurate with experience and skills.

Senior Associate: Police Executive Research Forum

Description:
Senior Associates in PERF's Management Services Division provide technical assistance and consulting services to policing agencies nationwide on a variety of management and organizational topics, from full-scale management audits and organizational development strategies to technical assistance focusing on a specific unit.

Qualifications:
An advanced degree is required. Applicants must have significant law enforcement experience; knowledge of best practices in community policing and problem-oriented policing; the ability to collect and analyze data; computer literacy; and exceptional multi-tasking ability. The position involves travel. Experience with a CALEA-accredited (Commission on Accreditation for Law Enforcement Agencies) police department is desirable.

Education:
A minimum master's degree is required for this position.

Preferred/Required Skills:
1. Good written and oral communication skills
2. Good interpersonal skills
3. Good research skills
4. Good analytical skills
5. Good computer skills

Training:
No specific agency training noted.

Grade Level(s): Not applicable

What to Expect:
1. Interview

Salary Range:
The salary range for this position is competitive and commensurate with qualifications and experience.

POSITIONS REQUIRING A DOCTORATE DEGREE

Criminologist/Social Scientist: RAND Corporation

Description:
The RAND Corporation is a non-profit think tank that strives to improve policy and decision- making through research and analysis. This position is for a mid-to-senior-level researcher interested in crime, delinquency, and public safety. RAND's Criminal Justice researchers often work in multidisciplinary teams, employ both quantitative and qualitative methodologies, and examine a variety of issues, including sentencing and corrections, violence and delinquency prevention, drug policy and treatment, terrorism, violence against women, policing, and community violence. The position can be located in either Santa Monica, California, or Arlington, Virginia.

Qualifications:
A Ph.D. in criminology, sociology, or related social science is required, with a minimum of five years research experience. Candidates must possess a strong publication record and the ability to work constructively within a collaborative environment, mentor junior researchers, and effectively lead interdisciplinary teams. Applications should include a cover letter, curriculum vitae, and writing sample.

Education:
A Ph.D. in criminology, sociology, or related social science is required for this position.

Preferred/Required Skills:
1. Excellent writing and communication skills
2. High level research skills
3. Excellent interpersonal skills

Training:
No specific agency/state training noted.

Grade Level(s): Not applicable

What to Expect:
1.   Interview

Salary Range:
The salary for this position is competitive.

Post-Doctoral Research Fellowships: George Mason University

Description:
One of the areas of research for which fellowships are available involves examining clinical, social, and developmental aspects of moral emotions for continued work on a longitudinal family study of moral emotions and behavioral adjustment (drug and alcohol use, safe sex, community service involvement, arrests and convictions, driving record, etc.).

Qualifications:
An earned Ph.D. is required for this position. Preferred applicants will have experience with complex longitudinal data sets and a strong background in developmental theory. Applicants must submit a curriculum vitae, statement of interests and research, and the names and contact information of three references.

Education:
A Ph.D. is required for this position.

Preferred/Required Skills:
1.   Strong research skills
2.   Quantitative skills
3.   Skill utilizing statistical software

Training:
No specific agency/state training noted.

Grade Level(s): Not applicable

What to Expect:
1.   Interview

Salary Range:
The salary for this position is commensurate with qualifications and experience.

*This example is for George Mason University. Salary and qualifications may vary by institution.

Program Director (Research): Caliber Associates

Description:
The Director shapes the strategic direction of research. Responsibilities include the leadership and development of a team of researchers working on multi-million dollar projects.

Qualifications:
Applicants should have a Ph.D., 15 or more years of experience, and should be a respected expert in the field with significant experience developing research programs and leading nationally recognized projects. Applicants should enclose cover letter and independently written and edited writing sample, along with salary requirements and resume.

Education:
A Ph.D. in criminology, public safety, sociology, or related discipline is required for this position.

Preferred/Required Skills:
1.   Excellent leadership skills
2.   Creativity in developing research projects
3.   Skill at directing funding activity
4.   Ability to oversee research and evaluation of projects

Training:
No specific agency/state training noted.

Grade Level(s): Not applicable

What to Expect:
1.   Interview

Salary Range:
The salary range for this position is competitive.

Project Director: Vera Institute of Justice

Description:
The project director leads a demonstration project that tests a new model of respite care for ungovernable or truant youth in the city's PINS (Persons in Need of Supervision) system. The project director is responsible for monitoring the results and changing the model to reflect lessons learned from early experience; negotiates the precise division of responsibilities between Vera and the provider; and manages the relationship so the program serves the interests of each organization and the PINS families. The project director supervises the respite staff of about twenty persons, oversees the budget, and speaks publicly regarding the project.

Qualifications:
Applicants must have a master's degree or Ph.D. The position requires experience working with adolescents, families, and governmental agencies. Applicants must be willing to work long hours, including during the night and on weekends.

Education:
An advanced degree is required for this position.

Preferred/Required Skills:
1.   Strong management skills
2.   Strong writing skills
3.   Strong public speaking skills

Training:
No specific agency/state training noted.

Grade Level(s): Not applicable

What to Expect:
1.   Interview

Salary Range:
The top salary for this position at Vera is $85,000 per year.

Research Fellowship: American Bar Foundation

Description:
ABF Research Fellows initiate, develop, conduct and publish their own and collaborative scholarly research funded through the ABF's financial resources or through grants made to individual projects by government agencies and private foundations.

Qualifications:
Candidates must have completed a law degree or a Ph.D. in a relevant discipline. Senior candidates must be able to demonstrate outstanding scholarship while junior candidates must demonstrate outstanding potential. Applications must include a cover letter, brief statement of current research activities and future plans, resume/curriculum vitae, four copies of the applicant's three leading publications (senior applicants) or other evidence of scholarship (junior applicants). All applicants should also provide two references to forward confidential letters of support directly to the Foundation.

Education:
A law degree or Ph.D. is required for this position.

Preferred/Required Skills:
1.   Outstanding research skills
2.   Excellent writing skills

Training:
No specific agency/state training noted.

Grade Level(s): Not applicable

What to Expect:
1.   Interview

Salary Range:
Salaries are competitive with those at leading research universities.

Senior Research Associate: Vera Institute of Justice

Description:
The Senior Research Associate will work closely with the Research Director, a team of existing research associates, and other staff throughout the Institute. On individual projects, the Senior Research Associate will serve as a project manager responsible for work in all phases of research, including research design, implementing research projects, conducting statistical analyses, making presentations, writing reports, administration, and supervising staff.

Qualifications:
Applicants must have a doctoral degree. Preference will be given to applicants with background and experience in quantitative methodology, program evaluation, writing research reports and articles, successful grant writing, and conducting research on substance abuse treatment for adolescents. Applicants should supply a curriculum vitae.

Education:
A Ph.D. is required for this position.

Preferred/Required Skills:
1.   Excellent writing skills
2.   Excellent research skills
3.   Grant writing skills

Training:
No specific agency/state training noted.

Grade Level(s): Not applicable

What to Expect:
1.   Interview

Salary Range:
The salary for this position is commensurate with experience and

qualifications.

PART FOUR
Academic Teaching Positions

TEACHING WITH A MASTER'S DEGREE
AT TWO YEAR COLLEGES

Community colleges vary widely in the way they are organized. Full-time teaching faculty at community colleges may either be ranked or unranked. For example, some large community colleges may rank teaching faculty similarly to four year institutions. Most community colleges have an unranked teaching structure whereby all professors are referred to as instructors or as teaching faculty. Regardless of whether the faculty is ranked or unranked, salaries will vary depending on education, experience, and qualifications. The following positions are models of two different community colleges.

Missouri Model: Teaching Faculty or Instructor

Description:
This model does not rank faculty members as Assistant Professor, Associate Professor, or Professor. All positions are referred to as instructors or teaching faculty. Full-time faculty members are usually required to teach five classes, advise students during office hours, and serve on committees which provide service to the college. The emphasis in community colleges is on excellence in teaching. There is no pressure to publish or procure grant funding, but publications may be considered a plus. The position generally entails a nine month contract, and may be tenure track or non tenure track.

Qualifications:
Applicants must have a master's degree in criminal justice or a related field. The position may require specialization in one or more areas. Applicants may be required to show proof of their legal right to work in the U.S. and must provide a resume, official transcript of graduate work, letters of recommendation, and references. If chosen from the pool of applicants for an interview, candidates for the position will be interviewed in person, and will be expected to teach a sample class in order to demonstrate their teaching ability.

Education:
A master's degree is required for this position.

Preferred/Required Skills:
1. High quality teaching skills
2. Extensive knowledge of subject matter
3. Ability to work independently
4. Good organizational skills
5. Good interpersonal skills

Training: Not applicable.

Rank: Full-time Faculty

What to Expect:
1. Personal interview
2. Provide demonstration of ability to teach

Salary Range:
Many of those teaching at the community college level are part-time instructors and are paid by the course. In Missouri, this would be from $1,800 to $2,000 per class. Full-time faculty with a master's degree would range from $35,000 to $42,000 in Kansas City.

*Salary and qualifications will vary and salary is negotiable.

California Model: Instructor, Assistant Professor, Associate Professor, Professor

Description:
A full-time teaching position at a community college that ranks its teaching faculty usually will require teaching five classes, holding office hours, serving on committees, and participating in student activities. Ranking is determined by the number of years of teaching experience and additional education which places professors at different salary steps corresponding with the ranks of Assistant Professor, Associate Professor, and Professor. Instructors are full-time, but on a probationary contract. Assistant professors and above are tenured faculty. The emphasis in community colleges that utilize ranking is on excellence in teaching. There is no pressure to publish or procure grant funding, and publications do not aid in promotion. The position generally entails a nine month contract.

Qualifications:
Proof of a master's degree in criminal justice or a related field is required, with the degree completed prior to appointment. The position may require specialization in one or more areas and commitment to quality teaching. Experience in community college teaching is desired. Applicants may be required to show proof of their legal right to work in the U.S. and must provide a resume that includes educational background, professional experience, and related personal development and accomplishments, plus official transcripts of graduate work, letters of recommendation, and references. If chosen from the pool of applicants for an interview, candidates for the position will be interviewed in person, and will be expected to teach a sample class in order to demonstrate their teaching ability.

Education:
A master's degree or A.B.D. (all but the dissertation completed) in criminal justice or a related field is required for this position.

Preferred/Required Skills:
1.   High quality teaching skills
2.   Extensive knowledge of subject matter
3.   Ability to work independently
4.   Good organizational skills
5.   Good interpersonal skills

Training: Not applicable

Rank: Full-time Faculty

What to Expect:
1.   Personal interview
2.   Provide demonstration of ability to teach

Salary Range:
The starting salary for this position is $44,000 to $64,000, based on education and teaching experience.

*Salary and qualifications will vary among colleges, and salary is negotiable.

TEACHING WITH A MASTER'S DEGREE
AT FOUR YEAR COLLEGES AND UNIVERSITIES

Instructor

Description:
This position is usually held by doctoral candidates to provide them with teaching experience while they finish their doctoral program. They teach introductory level courses as part of a graduate assistantship or fellowship. In most cases, instructors will teach one class per semester.

Qualifications:
This position requires a master's degree in criminal justice or a related field, and excellent progress in a Ph.D. program.

Education:
A master's degree is required for this position.

Preferred/Required Skills:
1.   Ability to teach effectively
2.   Extensive knowledge of subject matter
3.   Effective oral and writing skills
4.   Ability to work independently
5.   Good organizational skills
6.   Good interpersonal skills

Training:
Instructors may receive training in teaching skills as part of the assistantship or fellowship.

Rank: Instructor

Salary Range:
The salary range for this position is usually $10,000 to $20,000 per year for assistantships or fellowships.

Adjunct Professor

Description:
Adjunct Professors are hired on a part-time basis, per semester, to teach a class or several classes. This is a non-tenure track position, usually filled by an applicant that works full-time in another profession.

Qualifications:
Applicants must have proof of at least a master's degree in criminal justice or a related field, or a juris doctorate (law degree). They may be required to show proof of their legal right to work in the U.S. Applicants must provide a curriculum vitae, official transcript of graduate work, letters of recommendation, and references. If chosen from the pool of applicants for an interview, candidates for the position will be interviewed in person for the position, and may be expected to teach a sample class to demonstrate teaching ability.

Education:
A master's degree is required for this position. Applicants should be aware that more education increases the likelihood of advancement and promotion.

Preferred/Required Skills:
1.   Ability to teach effectively
2.   Extensive knowledge of subject matter
3.   Ability to work independently
4.   Good organizational skills
5.   Good interpersonal skills

Training: Not applicable

Rank: Adjunct

What to Expect:
1.   Personal interview
2.   Provide demonstration of ability to teach

Salary Range:
The salary range for this position is commensurate with qualifications, experience, and the needs of the college or university.

Visiting Professor

Description:
This is a teaching position at the college or university level that is temporary, usually for nine months. Visiting professors are usually at the rank of assistant professor. The position may have the possibility of promotion to a tenure track position if the department is impressed by the work of the visiting professor and funds become available. The position usually requires a teaching load of two to four classes in criminal justice or criminology per semester, plus research, grant funding efforts, and service to the college, profession, and community.

Qualifications:
The applicant must be A.B.D. (all but the dissertation completed), with the requirement that the Ph.D. be attained within a specified period of time. The position may require specialization in one or more areas; an active research agenda; potential or record of funded research activities; commitment to quality teaching; dedication to service to the institution through participation on institution-wide committees; service to the community through grant-funded projects or volunteer work; service to the profession through participation in academic conferences. Applicants may be required to show proof of their legal right to work in the U.S. Applicants must provide a curriculum vitae, official transcript of graduate work, letters of recommendation, and references. If chosen from the pool of applicants for an interview, candidates for the position will be interviewed in person, and may be expected to teach a sample class to demonstrate teaching ability.

Education:
The position requires that the applicant be A.B.D.

Preferred/Required Skills:
1.   Ability to teach effectively
2.   Ability to conduct original research and publish the results
3.   Ability to write grant proposals
4.   Ability to work independently
5.   Good organizational skills
6.   Good interpersonal skills

Training: Not applicable

Rank: Visiting Professor

What to Expect:
1. Personal interview
2. Provide demonstration of ability to teach

Salary Range:
The salary range for this position is commensurate with qualifications, experience, and the needs of the college or university.

TEACHING WITH A DOCTORATE DEGREE
AT TWO YEAR COLLEGES

Missouri Model: Teaching Faculty or Instructor

Description:
This model does not rank faculty members as Assistant Professor, Associate Professor, or Professor. All positions are referred to as instructors or teaching faculty. Full-time faculty members are usually required to teach five classes, advise students during office hours, and serve on committees which provide service to the college. The emphasis in community colleges is on excellence in teaching. There is no pressure to publish or procure grant funding, but publications may be considered a plus. The position generally entails a nine month contract, and may be tenure track or nontenure track.

Qualifications:
Applicants must have a Ph.D. in criminal justice or a related field, or be A.B.D. and finish within a specified period of time. The position requires commitment to quality teaching, and may require specialization in one or more areas. Applicants may be required to show proof of their legal right to work in the U.S. and must provide a resume, official transcript of graduate work, letters of recommendation, and references. If chosen from the pool of applicants for an interview, candidates for the position will be interviewed in person, and will be expected to teach a sample class in order to demonstrate their teaching ability.

Education:
A Ph.D. is required for this position.

Preferred/Required Skills:
1.　High quality teaching skills
2.　Extensive knowledge of subject matter
3.　Ability to work independently
4.　Good organizational skills
5.　Good interpersonal skills

Training: Not applicable

Rank: Full-time Faculty

What to Expect:
1.　Personal interview
2.　Provide demonstration of ability to teach

Salary Range:
Full-time faculty with Ph.D.'s have a salary range of $38,639 to $46,139 in Kansas City. Salary is commensurate with qualifications, experience, and the needs of the college. A Ph.D. allows the applicant to enter at a higher salary than an applicant with equivalent experience and a master's degree.

*Salary and qualifications will vary and salary is negotiable.

California Model: Instructor, Assistant Professor, Associate Professor, or Professor

Description:
A full-time teaching position at a community college that ranks its teaching faculty usually will require teaching five classes, holding office hours, serving on committees, and participating in student activities. Ranking is determined by the number of years of teaching experience and additional education which places professors at different salary steps corresponding with the ranks of Assistant Professor, Associate Professor, and Professor. Instructors are full-time, but on a probationary contract. Assistant professors and above are tenured faculty. The emphasis in community colleges that utilize ranking is on excellence in teaching. There is no pressure to publish or procure grant funding, and publications do not aid in promotion. The position generally entails a nine month contract.

Qualifications:

Proof of a Ph.D. in criminal justice or a related field is required, with the degree completed prior to appointment. The position may require specialization in one or more areas and commitment to quality teaching. Experience in community college teaching is desired. Applicants may be required to show proof of their legal right to work in the U.S. and must provide a resume that includes educational background, professional experience, and related personal development and accomplishments, plus official transcripts of graduate work, letters of recommendation, and references. If chosen from the pool of applicants for an interview, candidates for the position will be interviewed in person, and will be expected to teach a sample class in order to demonstrate their teaching ability.

Education:

A Ph.D. is required for this position.

Preferred/Required Skills:
1. High quality teaching skills
2. Extensive knowledge of subject matter
3. Ability to work independently
4. Good organizational skills
5. Good interpersonal skills

Training: Not applicable

Rank: Full-time Faculty

What to Expect:
1. Personal interview
2. Provide demonstration of ability to teach

Salary Range:

The starting salary for this position is $44,000 to $64,000, based on education and teaching experience.

*Salary and qualifications will vary among colleges, and salary is negotiable.

TEACHING WITH A DOCTORATE DEGREE
AT FOUR YEAR COLLEGES AND UNIVERSITIES

Visiting Professor

Description:
This is a teaching position at the college or university level that is temporary, usually for nine months. Visiting Professors are usually at the rank of assistant professor. The position may have the possibility of promotion to a tenure track position if the department is impressed by the work of the visiting professor and funds become available. The position usually requires a teaching load of two to four classes in criminal justice or criminology per semester, plus research, grant funding efforts, and service to the college, profession, and community.

Qualifications:
The applicant must be at least A.B.D. (all but dissertation completed) with the requirement that the Ph.D. be attained within a specified period of time. The position may require specialization in one or more areas; an active research agenda; potential or record of funded research activities; commitment to quality teaching; dedication to service to the college through participation on college-wide committees; service to the community through grant funded projects or volunteer work; service to the profession through participation in academic association conferences. Applicants may be required to show proof of their legal right to work in the U.S. Applicants must provide a curriculum vitae, official transcript of graduate work, letters of recommendation, and references. If chosen from the pool of applicants for an interview, candidates for the position will be interviewed in person, and may be expected to teach a sample class to demonstrate teaching ability.

Education:
The position requires that applicants be A.B.D. or have a Ph.D.

Preferred/Required Skills:
1.   Ability to teach effectively
2.   Ability to conduct original research and publish the results
3.   Ability to write grant proposals
4.   Ability to work independently
5.   Good organizational skills

6.   Good interpersonal skills

Training: Not applicable

Rank: Visiting Professor

What to Expect:
1.   Personal interview
2.   Provide demonstration of ability to teach

Salary Range:
The salary range for this position is commensurate with qualifications, experience, and the needs of the college or university.

Assistant Professor (Non-Tenure Track)

Description:
This is an entry level position at a four year college or university. Assistant Professors who are not tenure track will teach four classes per semester, which is more than tenure track professors. They will not have the same pressure to publish or procure grants as tenure track positions, since the position does not have the possibility of job security that accompanies a tenure track position. They may be expected to advise students in addition to their teaching load.

Qualifications:
Either A.B. D. (all but the dissertation completed) or a Ph.D. in criminal justice or a related field is required. Oftentimes, the degree must be completed prior to appointment. The position may require specialization in one or more areas and a commitment to quality teaching. Applicants must show proof of a Ph.D. in criminal justice or a related field. They may be required to show proof of their legal right to work in the U.S. Applicants must provide a curriculum vitae, official transcript of graduate work, letters of recommendation, and references. If chosen from the pool of applicants for an interview, candidates for the position will be interviewed in person, and will be expected to teach a sample class to demonstrate teaching ability.

Education:
Applicants must be A.B.D. or have a Ph.D.

Preferred/Required Skills:
1.   Ability to teach effectively
2.   Extensive knowledge of subject matter
3.   Excellent oral and writing skills
4.   Ability to work independently
5.   Good organizational skills
6.   Good interpersonal skills

Training: Not applicable

Rank: Assistant Professor

What to Expect:
1.   Personal interview
2.   Demonstration of ability to teach

Salary Range:
The salary range for this position is commensurate with qualifications, experience, and the needs of the college or university.

Assistant Professor (Tenure Track)

Description:
This is an entry level position at a four year college or university. In most cases, Assistant Professors will have a teaching load of two or three classes in criminal justice or criminology. They will also be expected to provide service to the college or university by serving on committees and advising students. Research and publication of the results in academic journals is expected on a regular basis. Assistant Professors are also expected to provide service to the community through volunteer work or grant-funded projects, and service to the wider academic community by attending conferences. This is a nine month position with the possibility of promotion to Associate Professor after a specified period of years (usually five years). Tenured professors cannot be fired without justifiable cause.

Qualifications:
A Ph.D. or A.B.D. in criminal justice or a related field is required, usually with the degree completed prior to appointment. The position may require specialization in one or more areas; an active research agenda; potential for obtaining research grants; commitment to quality teaching; and dedication to service to the college, profession, and community. Applicants must show proof of a Ph.D. in criminal justice or a related field. They may be required to show proof of their legal right to work in the U.S. Applicants must provide a curriculum vitae, writing sample, official transcript of graduate work, letters of recommendation, and references. If chosen from the pool of applicants for an interview, candidates for the position will be interviewed in person, and will be expected to teach a sample class to demonstrate teaching ability.

Education:
Applicants must be A.B.D. or have a Ph.D., depending on the college or university.

Preferred/Required Skills:
1.   Ability to teach effectively
2.   Extensive knowledge of subject matter
3.   Excellent oral and writing skills
4.   Ability to conduct original research projects and publish the results
5.   Ability to write grant proposals
6.   Good interpersonal skills

Training: Not applicable

Rank: Assistant Professor

What to Expect:
1.   Personal interview
2.   Provide demonstration of ability to teach

Salary Range:
Median salaries for assistant professors in selected areas of the U.S. are: Sacramento, CA: $63,493; Des Moines, IA: $58,386; Jackson, MS: $55,371; Atlanta, GA: $58,928; Boston, MA: $64,688.

*Salary and qualifications will vary and salary is negotiable.

Associate Professor

Description:
Associate Professors will usually have a teaching load of two classes in criminal justice or criminology. They will also be expected to provide service to the college or university by serving on college-wide committees and assisting students by participating on thesis and dissertation committees. Associate Professors are also expected to provide service to the community through grant-funded projects or volunteer work, and to provide service to the wider academic community by participating in conferences and holding elected positions in academic associations. Conducting research and publishing the results in academic journals is expected on a regular basis. This is a nine month position with the possibility of promotion after a specified number of years.

Qualifications:
A Ph.D. in criminal justice or a related field is required, with about five years teaching experience at the level of Assistant Professor, depending on the policies of the respective college or university. The position may require specialization in one or more areas; regular publications in scholarly journals; potential or record of funded research activities; record of quality teaching; demonstrated service to the college, profession, and community. Applicants must show proof of a Ph.D. in criminal justice or a related field. They may be required to show proof of their legal right to work in the U.S. Applicants must provide a curriculum vitae, a reprint of a published work, official transcript of graduate work, letters of recommendation, and references. If chosen from the pool of applicants for an interview, candidates for the position will be interviewed in person, and will be expected to teach a sample class to demonstrate teaching ability.

Education:
A Ph.D. in criminal justice or a related field is required for this position.

Preferred/Required Skills:
1.   Ability to teach effectively
2.   Extensive knowledge of subject matter
3.   Excellent oral and writing skills
4.   Ability to conduct original research projects and gain publications
5.   Ability to write effective grant proposals
6.   Good interpersonal skills

Training: Not applicable

Rank: Associate Professor

What to Expect:
1. Personal interview
2. Provide demonstration of ability to teach

Salary Range:
Median salaries for associate professors in selected areas of the U.S. are:
Sacramento, CA: $78,572; Des Moines, IA: $72,252; Jackson, MS: $68,521; Atlanta, GA: $72,923; Boston, MA: $80,051.

*Salary and qualifications will vary and salary is negotiable.

Professor

Description:
This is a senior teaching position. A Professor will usually teach one or two classes, serve on thesis and dissertation committees, and continue to conduct research, write, and publish manuscripts. Professors provide service to the college or university, to the community, and also to the profession by participating in conferences and holding leadership positions in academic associations.

Qualifications:
A Professor must have a Ph.D. in criminal justice or a related field, has usually been granted tenure, typically has at least ten years of teaching experience, and has been promoted from the rank of associate professor. He or she usually has authored at least one published book in addition to numerous, regular journal publications. Outstanding achievements in teaching, service to the community through major projects in their specialized area, or successful grant writing, will aid in fulfilling requirements. A Professor usually has a regional reputation. Applicants must show proof of a Ph.D. in criminal justice or a related field. They may be required to show proof of their legal right to work in the U.S. Applicants must provide a curriculum vitae, a reprint of a published work, official transcript of graduate work, letters of recommendation, and references. If chosen from the pool of applicants for an interview,

candidates for the position will be interviewed in person, and will be expected to teach a sample class to demonstrate teaching ability.

Education:
A Ph.D. in criminal justice or a related field is required for this position.

Preferred/Required Skills:
1.   Ability to teach effectively
2.   Ability to conduct original research projects and publish results in refereed journals
3.   Creativity and ability to write and gain publication of book manuscripts
4.   Ability to write effective grant proposals
5.   Good interpersonal skills

Training: Not applicable

Rank: Professor

What to Expect:
1.   Personal interview
2.   Provide demonstration of ability to teach

Salary Range:
Median salaries for full professors in selected areas of the U.S. are: Sacramento, CA: $101,901; Des Moines, IA: $93,704; Jackson, MS: $88,866; Atlanta, GA: $94,575; Boston, MA: $103,819.

*Salary and qualifications will vary and salary is negotiable.

Distinguished Professor

Description:
This is not a formal title, but occasionally a job announcement will appear asking for a distinguished professor. Few professors reach this level, as distinguished professors are those scholars with a national reputation for research and scholarship. The successful applicant will be hired as a tenured Professor. A distinguished professor will spend most or all of his or her time doing research and writing, and will teach one class at the

most.

Qualifications:
Distinguished Professors hold the rank of Professor and must have a prolific publishing record and a strong agenda for continued research productivity. They have written many books, in addition to numerous journal articles. Their names are familiar to anyone in the field, and their work is considered important enough that it is cited regularly by others in the profession. They must provide a curriculum vitae.

Education:
A Ph.D. is required for this position.

Preferred/Required Skills:
1.   Excellent research skills
2.   High degree of creativity
3.   High degree of motivation
4.   Excellent writing skills

Training: Not applicable

Rank: Professor

What to Expect:
1.   Presentation of research agenda

Salary Range:
The salary range for this position is $90,000 and up, depending on the institution, and is highly negotiable.

Professor Emeritus

Description:
This is an honorary position and will not be advertised. A Professor in this position has retired, but because of the respect of his or her colleagues, has been given this status in order to teach on a part-time basis. A Professor Emeritus will usually teach one or two classes, and will retain an office in the department, but will not be expected to conduct research or publish.

Qualifications:
The requirement for this status is to be at the rank of a Professor, to be highly respected by colleagues in the department, and to be at retirement age.

Education:
A Ph.D. in criminal justice or a related field is required for this title.

Skills: Not applicable

Training: Not applicable

Rank: Professor

Salary Range:
The salary range for this position depends on the university.

ADDRESSES OF SOME COLLEGES AND UNIVERSITIES

Alabama

Alabama State University
Department of Sociology and Criminal Justice
207 Beverly Hall
915 South Jackson Street
Montgomery, AL 36101-0271
(334) 229-4366/4120

Auburn University at Montgomery
Department of Justice and Public Safety
P.O. Box 244023
Montgomery, Al 36124-4023
(334) 244-3000

Troy State University
Department of Criminal Justice and Social Sciences
Troy, AL 36082
(334) 670-3000

University of Alabama - Birmingham
Department of Justice Sciences
1530 3rd Ave. South
Birmingham, AL 35294-1150

University of Alabama
Department of Criminal Justice
Box 870320
Tuscaloosa, AL 35487-0320
(205) 348-7795

University of South Alabama
Department of Political Science and Criminal Justice
Humanities Bldg. #226
Mobile, AL 36688-0002
(251) 460-7161

Alaska
> University of Alaska - Anchorage
> Justice Center
> 3211 Providence Drive
> Anchorage, AK 9508
> (907) 786-1810
>
> University of Alaska - Fairbanks
> Justice Department
> 6th Floor Gruening Building
> University of Alaska, Fairbanks
> Fairbanks, AK 99775
> (907) 474-5500

Arkansas
> University of Arkansas - Little Rock
> College of Professional Programs
> 2801 South University Avenue
> Little Rock, AR 72204-1099
> (501) 569-3195
>
> University of Arkansas at Pine Bluff
> Department of Social and Behavioral Sciences
> Pine Bluff, AS 71611
> (870) 575-8171

California
> California State University at Fresno
> Department of Criminology
> 2225 E. San Ramon, MS/MF 104
> Fresno, CA 93740- 8029
> (559) 278-2305
>
> California State University at Long Beach
> Criminal Justice Department
> 1250 Bellflower Boulevard
> Long Beach, CA 90840
> (562) 985- 4738

California State University at Sacramento
Criminal Justice Division
6000 J Street
Sacramento, CA 95819
(916) 278-6487

California State University at San Bernardino
Department of Criminal Justice
5500 University Parkway
San Bernardino, CA 92407
(909) 880-5508

Sonoma State University
Department of Criminal Justice Administration
1801 E. Catati Avenue
Rohnert Park, CA 94928-3609
(707) 664-2934

University of California - Irvine
School of Social Ecology
Department of Criminology, Law and Society
Room 2340, Social Ecology II
Irvine, CA 92697
(949) 824-5575

Colorado
University of Colorado - Denver
Graduate School of Public Affairs
P.O. Box 173364
Campus Box 142
Denver, CO 80217-3364
(303) 556-5970

University of Denver
Department of Sociology
2000 E. Asbury Avenue, Room SH 446
Denver, CO 80208-2948
(303) 871-2948

Connecticut

Central Connecticut State University
Department of Criminology and Criminal Justice
Room 454 Vance Academic Center
New Britain, CT 06050-4010
(860) 832-3005

University of New Haven
Department of Criminal Justice
300 Orange Avenue
West Haven, CT 06516
(800) 342-5864

Western Connecticut State University
Division of Justice and Law Administration
349 Westside Campus
181 White Street
Danbury, Connecticut 06810
(203) 837-8340

Delaware

University of Delaware
Department of Sociology and Criminal Justice
322 Smith Hall
Newark, DE 19716
(302) 831-2581

District of Columbia

American University
Department of Justice, Law and Society
Ward Circle Building
4400 Massachusetts Avenue NW
Washington, D.C. 20016-8043
(202) 885-2948

George Washington University
Department of Sociology
801 22nd St. NW, Suite 409
Washington, D.C. 20052
(202) 994-6345

Florida

Florida Atlantic University
Department of Criminology and Criminal Justice
777 Glades Road
Boca Raton, FL 33341
(561) 297-3240

Florida State University
School of Criminology and Criminal Justice
Hecht House 634 West Call Street
Tallahassee, FL 32306-1127
(850) 644-4050

University of Central Florida
Criminal Justice and Legal Studies
College of Health and Public Affairs
HPA I Suite 311
Orlando, FL 32816-1600
(407) 823-2603

University of North Florida
Department of Sociology, Anthropology and Criminal Justice
4567 St. Johns Bluff Road South
Jacksonville, FL 32224-2666
(904) 620-2850

University of South Florida
Department of Criminology
4202 E. Fowler Avenue, SOC 107
Tampa, FL 33620-8100
(813) 974-2815

Georgia

Albany State University
Department of Criminal Justice
Albany, GA 31705
(229) 430-4864

Armstrong Atlantic University
Department of Criminal Justice, Social, and Political Science
11935 Abercorn Street
Savannah, GA 31419
(912)-927-5277

Clark-Atlanta State University
Department of Criminal Justice Administration
219 Oglethorpe Hall
223 James P. Brawley Drive SW
Atlanta, GA 30314
(404) 880-6659

Georgia State University
Department of Criminal Justice
1281 Urban Life Center
Atlanta, GA 30302
(404) 651-3515

Valdosta State University
Department of Sociology, Anthropology and Criminal Justice
1500 N. Patterson St.
Valdosta, GA 31698
(800) 618-1878

Hawaii

Chaminade University of Honolulu
Department of Criminal Justice
3140 Wailae Avenue
Honolulu, HI 96816-1578
(808) 739-4614

University of Hawaii at Hilo
Administration of Justice
200 W. Kawili Street
Hilo, HI 96720-4091
(808) 974-7461

Idaho

Boise State University
Department of Criminal Justice Administration
1910 University Drive
Boise, ID 83725-1955
(800) 824-7017 ext. 307

Lewis-Clark State College
Social Sciences Division
500 8th Avenue
Lewiston, ID 83501
(208) 792-2291

University of Idaho
Department of Sociology, Anthropology and Justice Studies
Phinney Hall
Moscow, ID 83844-1110
(208) 885-6751

Illinois

Chicago State University
Department of Criminal Justice
9501 South King Drive
HWH 329
Chicago, IL 60628
(773) 995-2108

Illinois State University
Department of Criminal Justice Sciences
Schroeder 401
Normal, IL 61790
(309) 438-7617

Northern Illinois University
Division of Public Administration
DeKalb, IL 60115
(815) 753-0184

Southern Illinois University at Carbondale
Department of Administration of Justice
Mailcode 4504
Carbondale, IL 62901-4504
(618) 453-5701

University of Illinois at Chicago
Department of Criminal Justice
1007 West Harrison Street
M/C 141
Chicago, IL 60607
(312) 413-3030

Western Illinois University
Department of Law Enforcement and Justice Administration
Stipes Hall 403
1 University Drive
Macomb, IL 61455
(309) 298-1038

Indiana

Indiana University at Bloomington
Department of Criminal Justice
Sycamore Hall 302
Bloomington, IN 47405
(812) 855-9325

Indiana University Purdue University- Indianapolis
School of Public and Environmental Affairs
801 West Michigan Street
Indianapolis, IN 46202
(877) 292-9321

Indiana University Northwest
School of Public and Environmental Affairs and Political Science
3400 Broadway Avenue
Gary, IN 46408
(219) 980-6500

Indiana State University
Department of Criminology
Holmstedt Hall 208-210
Terre Haute, IN 47809
(812) 237-2192

Iowa

Buena Vista University
Department of Criminal Justice
610 West 4th Street
Storm Lake, IA 50588
(800) 383-2821

St. Ambrose University
518 West Locust Street
Davenport, IA 52803
(563) 333-6096

University of Northern Iowa
Department of Sociology/Anthropology/Criminology
Baker Hall 356
Cedar Falls, IA 50614
(319) 273-2786

Upper Iowa University
Social Sciences Program
P.O. Box 1857
605 Washington Street
Fayette, IA 52142-1857
(800) 553-4150

Kansas

Washburn University
Department of Criminal Justice
School of Applied Studies
1700 SW College Avenue
Topeka, KS 66621
(785) 231-1010 ext. 1411

Wichita State University
School of Community Affairs
Criminal Justice Program
1845 N. Fairmount-Campus Box 135
Wichita, KS 67260-0135
(316) 978-7200

Kentucky

Eastern Kentucky University
College of Justice and Safety
354 Stratton Building
521 Lancaster Avenue
Richmond, KY 40475-3102
(859) 622-3565

Morehead State University
Department of Sociology, Social Work and Criminology
Rader Hall
Morehead, KY 40351
(606) 783-2656

University of Louisville
Department of Justice Administration
Brigman Hall, Rm. 206
Louisville, KY 40292
(502) 852-0382

Louisiana

Grambling State University
Department of Criminal Justice
Grambling, LA 71245
(318) 274-2526

St. John's University
Criminal Justice Program
31916 University Circle
Springfield, LA 70462
(225) 294-2129

Southern University at New Orleans
Department of Criminal Justice
202 Multi-Purpose Building
6400 Press Drive
New Orleans, LA 70126
(504) 284-5478

University of Louisiana at Monroe
Department of Criminal Justice
700 University Avenue
Monroe, LA 71209
(318) 342-1440

Maine

Southern Maine University
P.O. Box 9300
Portland, ME 04104-9300
(207) 780-4105

University of Maine - Presque Isle
Department of Psychology, Social Work and Criminal Justice
207 Normal Hall
181 Maine Street
Presque Isle, ME 04769-2888
(207) 768-9465

Maryland

Coppin State College
Department of Criminal Justice and Law Enforcement
Building G5, Room 831
2500 W. North Avenue
Baltimore, MD 21216-3698
(410) 951-3050

University of Baltimore
Division of Criminology, Criminal Justice and Social Policy
1420 N. Charles Street
Baltimore, MD 21201
(410) 837-6084

University of Maryland - College Park
Department of Criminology and Criminal Justice
Samuel J. Le Frak Hall
College Park, MD 20742
(301) 405-4699

University of Maryland Eastern Shore
Department of Criminal Justice
Criminal Justice Building
Princess Anne, MD 21853
(410) 651-6578/6582

Massachusetts
Northeastern University
College of Criminal Justice
204 Churchill Hall
Boston, MA 02115
(617) 373-3327

Suffolk University
Department of Sociology
Goldberg Building
56 Temple Street
Boston, MA 02114
(617) 573-8485

University of Massachusetts at Amherst
Department of Legal Studies
131 Country Circle
221 Hampshire House
Amherst, MA 01003
(413) 545-0021

University of Massachusetts at Boston
Criminal Justice Center
Wheatley, 4th Floor
100 Morissey Boulevard.
Boston, MA 0215-3393
(617) 287-7100

University of Massachusetts at Lowell
Department of Criminal Justice
1 University Avenue
Lowell, MA 01854
(987) 934-4120

Westfield State College
Department of Criminal Justice
Westfield, MA 01086
(413) 572-5309

Michigan

Eastern Michigan University
Department of Sociology, Anthropology and Criminology
712 Pray-Harrold
Ypsilanti, MI 48197
(734) 487-0012

Ferris State University
School of Criminal Justice
509 Bishop Hall
1349 Cramer Circle
Big Rapids, MI 49307

Grand Valley State University
School of Criminal Justice
401 W. Fulton
Grand Rapids, MI 49504
(616) 336-7132

Michigan State University
School of Criminal Justice
506 Baker Hall
East Lansing, MI 48824-1024
(517) 355-2197

Northern Michigan University
Department of Criminal Justice
Walter F. Gries Hall Room 110
1401 Presque Isle Avenue
Marquette, MI 49855
(906) 227-2660

Minnesota

Bemidji State University
Department of Criminal Justice
1500 Birchmont Drive
Bemidji, MN 56601-2699
(218) 755-2000

Minnesota State University - Mankato
Political Science/Law Enforcement Department
Morris Hall 109
Mankato, MN 56001
(507) 389-2721

Minnesota State University - Moorhead
Department of Sociology and Criminal Justice
Lommen 102
1104 7th Avenue South
Moorhead, MN 56563
1 800 593-7246

St. Cloud State University
Department of Criminal Justice Studies
257 Stewart Hall
720 4th Avenue South
St. Cloud, MN 56301-4498
(320) 255-4101

Mississippi

Delta State University
Criminal Justice Program
Kethley 203 A
Cleveland, MS 38733
(800) 468-6378

Mississippi College
Administration of Justice
Box 4006
Clinton, MS 39058
(601) 925-3221

Mississippi Valley State University
Department of Criminal Justice
14000 Highway 82 West
Itta Bena, MS 38941
(662) 254-3364

University of Southern Mississippi
Department of Criminal Justice
Box 5127
Hattiesburg, MS 39406
(601) 266-4509

Missouri

Central Missouri State University
Criminal Justice Department
Warrensburg, MO 64093
(660) 543-4950

Drury University
Department of Behavioral Sciences
900 N. Benton Avenue
Springfield, MO 65802
(417) 873-7306

University of Missouri-Kansas City
Department of Sociology/Criminal Justice and Criminology
208 Haag Hall
5100 Rockhill Road
Kansas City, MO 64110-2499
(816) 235-1116

University of Missouri - St. Louis
Department of Criminology and Criminal Justice
324 Lucas Hall
800 Natural Bridge Road
St. Louis, MO 63121-4499
(314) 516-5031

Southeast Missouri State University
Department of Sociology and Anthropology
1 University Plaza
Cape Girardeau, MO 63701

Nebraska

University of Nebraska at Lincoln
Criminal Justice Program
Lincoln, NE 68588
(402) 472-7211

University of Nebraska at Omaha
Department of Criminal Justice
Durham Science Center Room 208
6001 Dodge St.
Omaha, NE 68182-0149
(402) 554-2610

University of Nebraska at Kearney
Department of Criminal Justice
Founders Hall
Kearney, NE 68849
(308) 865-8510

Nevada

University of Nevada - Las Vegas
Department of Criminal Justice
4505 Maryland Parkway
Las Vegas, NV 89154-5009
(702) 895-0238

University of Nevada at Reno
Department of Criminal Justice/214
Reno, NV 89557-0026
(775) 784-6164

New Jersey

New Jersey City University
Criminal Justice P220
2039 Kennedy Boulevard
Jersey City, NJ 07305-1597
(201) 200-3492

Rutgers University - Camden
Department of Sociology, Anthropology and Criminal Justice
311 N. 5th Street
Camden, NJ 08102-1405
(856) 225-6470

Rutgers University-Newark
School of Criminal Justice
249 University Avenue
Newark, NJ 07102
(973) 353-3292

Seton Hall University
Department of Criminal Justice
Arts and Sciences Hall
400 So. Orange Avenue
South Orange, NJ 07079
(973) 761-9108

New Mexico

Eastern New Mexico University
Psychology, Sociology, Criminal Justice and Political Science
ENMU Station 35
Portales, NM 88130
(505) 562-2045

New Mexico State University
Department of Criminal Justice
P.O. Box 3001
Las Cruces, NM 88001
(505) 646-3316

New York

The City University of New York (CUNY)
John Jay College of Criminal Justice
899 Tenth Avenue
New York, NY 10019
(212) 237-8000

Iona College
Criminal Justice Department
715 North Avenue
New Rochelle, NY 10801-1890
(914) 633-2000

Long Island University - Brentwood Campus
School of Public Service
100 Second Avenue
Brentwood, NY 11717
(631) 273-5112

Long Island University - C.W. Post Campus
Department of Criminal Justice
720 Northern Boulevard
Brookville, NY 11548
(516) 299-2000

Niagara University
Department of Criminal Justice
Niagara, NY 14109
(716) 286-8080

State University of New York - Albany
School of Criminal Justice
135 Western Avenue
Albany, NY 12222
(518) 442-5210

State University of New York - Buffalo
Interdisciplinary Degree Programs
641 Baldy Hall
Buffalo, NY 14260-1040
(716) 645-2245

North Carolina

Appalachian State University
Department of Political Science and Criminal Justice
P.O. Box 32107
Boone, NC 28608-2107
(828) 262-3085

East Carolina University
School of Social Work and Criminal Justice Studies
Ragsdale Building
Greenville, NC 27858-4353
(252) 328-4383

North Carolina Central University
Department of Criminal Justice
301 Whiting - Criminal Justice Bldg.
Durham, NC 27707
(919) 560-6280

University of North Carolina at Charlotte
Department of Criminal Justice
9201 University City Boulevard
Charlotte, NC 28223-0001
(704) 687-2562

University of North Carolina at Greensboro
Department of Sociology
Greensboro, NC 27402
(336) 334-5295

North Dakota
Minot State University
Department of Criminal Justice
500 University West
Minot, ND 58707
(701) 858-3303

University of North Dakota
Criminal Justice Studies
Grand Forks, ND 58202
(701) 777-2011

Ohio
Bowling Green State University
Criminal Justice Program
Bowling Green, OH 43403
(419) 372-2326

Kent State University
Department of Justice Studies
113 Bowman Hall
Kent, OH 44242-0001
(330) 672-2775

Tiffin University
School of Criminal Justice
155 Miami Street
Tiffin, OH 44883
(419) 448-3292

University of Cincinnati
Division of Criminal Justice
Student Services Center
P.O. Box 210002
Cincinnati, OH 45221-0389
(513) 556-2336

Xavier University
Department of Criminal Justice
154 Cohen Center
3800 Victory Parkway
Cincinnati, OH 45207
(513) 745-3518

Youngstown State University
Department of Criminal Justice
One University Plaza
Youngstown, OH 44555
(330) 742-3279

Oklahoma

East Central University
Department of Human Resources
Ada, OK 74820
(580) 310-5400

Northwestern Oklahoma State University
Department of Social and Community Services
709 Oklahoma Boulevard
Alva, OK 73717
(580) 327-8521

University of Central Oklahoma
Department of Sociology, Criminal Justice, and Substance Abuse
Studies
100 N. University Drive
Edmond, OK 73034
(405) 974-5520

Oregon

Portland State University
Administration of Justice Division
Mark O. Hatfield School of Government
P.O. Box 751
Portland, OR 97207-0751
(800) 547-8887

Western Oregon University
Criminal Justice Department HSS 224
345 N. Monmouth Avenue
Monmouth, OR 97361
(503) 838-8358

Pennsylvania

California University of Pennsylvania
Department of Justice Studies
250 University Avenue
California, PA 15419
(724) 938-4000

Indiana University of Pennsylvania
Criminology Department
G-1 McElhaney Hall
441 North Walk
Indiana, PA 15705
(724) 357-2720

Mercyhurst College
Department of Criminal Justice PRES 122
501 E. 38th Street
Erie, PA 16546
(814) 824-2328

Pennsylvania State University - Harrisburg
Criminal Justice Program
School of Public Affairs
777 W. Harrisburg Pike
Middletown, PA 17057
(717) 948-6319

Pennsylvania State University - University Park
Crime, Law, and Justice Program
Department of Sociology
211 Oswald Tower
University Park, PA 16804
(814) 863-8490

Shippensburg University
Department of Criminal Justice
1871 Old Main Drive
Shippensburg, PA 17257
(717) 277-1558

Saint Joseph's University
Criminal Justice Department
131 Villiger
5600 City Avenue
Philadelphia, PA 19131
(610) 660-1680

Temple University
Department of Criminal Justice
Gladfelter Hall, 5th Floor
1115 W. Berks Street
Philadelphia, PA 19122
(215) 204-7918

Villanova University
Criminal Justice Program
204 St. Augustine Center
800 Lancaster Avenue
Villanova, PA 19085
(610) 519-4600

Rhode Island
Roger Williams University
School of Justice Studies
1 Old Ferry Road
Bristol, RI 02809
(401) 254-3021

Salve Regina University
Administration of Justice
McAuley Hall Room 314
100 Ochre Point Avenue
Newport, RI 02840-4192
(401) 847-3277

South Carolina

The Citadel
Department of Political Science and Criminal Justice
171 Moultrie Street
Charleston, SC 29409
(843) 953-5072

University of South Carolina - Columbia
Department of Criminology and Criminal Justice
Columbia, SC 29208
(803) 777-7097

Tennessee

East Tennessee State University
Department of Criminal Justice and Criminology
201 Rogers Stout Hall
Box 70267
Johnson City, TN 37614-0054
(423) 439-5346

Middle Tennessee State University
Department of Criminal Justice Administration
1421 E. Main Street
P.O. Box 238
Murfreesboro, TN 37132
(615) 898-2630

Tennessee State University
Department of Criminal Justice
3500 John A. Merritt Boulevard
Nashville, TN 37209
(615) 963-5000

University of Memphis
Department of Criminology and Criminal Justice
309 McCord Hall
Memphis, TN 38152
(901) 678-2737

University of Tennessee - Chattanooga
School of Social and Community Services/Department 3203
615 McCallie Avenue
Chattanooga, TN 37403-2598
(423) 755-4135

Texas

St. Mary's University
Department of Criminal Justice
1 Camino Santa Maria
San Antonio, TX 78230
1 800 367-7868

Sam Houston State University
College of Criminal Justice
George J. Beto Criminal Justice Center
1803 Ave. I
Huntsville, TX 77341
(936) 294-1635

Southwest Texas State University
Department of Criminal Justice
Hines Academic Center Room 120
601 University Drive
San Marcos, TX 78666
(512) 245-2174

Sul Ross State University
Department of Criminal Justice
Morelock Academic Building, Room 109A
P.O. Box C-12
Alpine, TX 79832
(915) 837-8166

Tarleton State University - Central Texas
Department of Social Work, Sociology, and Criminal Justice
Box T-0665
Stephenville, TX 76402
(254) 968-9024

University of North Texas
Department of Criminal Justice
359 Chilton Hall
Denton, TX 76203-5130
(940) 565-2562

University of Texas at Arlington
Criminology and Criminal Justice Department
701 S. Nedderman Drive
Arlington, TX 76019
(817) 272-2011

University of Texas at San Antonio
Department of Criminal Justice
DB 4.112 B
501 W. Durango Boulevard
San Antonio, TX 78207
(210) 458-2535

Utah

Weber State University
Department of Criminal Justice
3850 University Circle
Ogden, UT 84408
(801) 626-6000

Virginia

George Mason University
Administration of Justice
10900 University Boulevard
Fairfax, VA 22030
(703) 993-8315

Radford University
Department of Criminal Justice
397 Adams Street
P.O. Box 69734
Radford, VA 24142
(540) 831-6161

University of Richmond
Department of Criminal Justice
28 Westhampton Way
Richmond, VA 23173
(804) 289-8070

Virginia Commonwealth University
Department of Criminal Justice
816 W. Franklin Street
P.O. Box 842017
Richmond, VA 23284-2017
(804) 828-1050

Virginia State University
Department of Sociology, Social Work and Criminal Justice
Petersburg, VA 23806
(804) 524-5000

Virginia Union University
Department of Criminology/Criminal Justice
1500 N. Lombardy Street
Richmond, VA 23220
(804) 257-5600

Washington

Gonzaga University
Department of Sociology
Criminal Justice Program
502 E. Boone Avenue
Spokane, WA 99258
(509) 323-6791

Washington State University
Department of Political Science/Program in Criminal Justice
P.O. Box 644880
801 Johnson Tower
Pullman, WA 99164-4880
(509) 335-2544

West Virginia
Marshall University
Criminal Justice Department
1 John Marshall Drive
Huntington, WV 25755-2662

West Virginia State University
Department of Criminal Justice
P.O. Box 1000
Institute, WV 25112
(304) 766-3221

Wisconsin
Marquette University
Department of Social and Cultural Sciences
Criminology and Law Studies Program
Lalumiere Hall
P.O. Box 1881
Milwaukee, WI 53201-1881
(414) 288-6838

University of Wisconsin - La Crosse
Department of Sociology and Archaeology
435 Carl Wimberly Hall
La Crosse, WI 54601
(608) 785-8457

University of Wisconsin - Milwaukee
Helen Bader School of Social Welfare
P.O. Box 786
Milwaukee, WI 53201
(414) 229-4851

University of Wisconsin - Parkside
Criminal Justice Department
Molinaro 362
900 Wood Road
Kenosha, WI 53141-2000
(262) 595-3416

Wyoming
University of Wyoming
Criminal Justice
P.O. Box 3197
Laramie, WY 82071-3197
(307) 766-2988

PART FIVE

Interviews from the Field:
In Their Own Words

INTERVIEWEE NUMBER 1
Name Optional: Jennie
Position: **Professor of Criminal Justice**
Number of Years: **10**

Q. How many hours a week do you typically work?
A. 50, and that's being conservative.

Q. How many years do you have to work before retirement?
A. Seventeen before I am eligible.

Q. Does your position allow you quality time with your family?
A. I have no family here. I am single and live alone.

Q. Does your current position allow for promotion?
A. No, I am a full Professor.

Q. What about location? Did you have a choice of where you would work?
A. Yes.

Q. What is the level of risk associated with your job?
A. Very low.

Q. What personality traits do you believe are important for this position?
A. I cannot answer; I am unsure about that.

Q. What does your daily routine consist of?
A. In academia, it varies. Generally, you teach, go to meetings, and you write. You talk to students. It just depends. It varies, it really does.

Q. What do you like best about your job?
A. I like the autonomy, I like that it makes a difference. I like students. I like watching them grow academically and giving them support. I like working with colleagues in scholarly pursuits. I like working with agencies and the opportunities that academia presents.

Q. What do you like least about your job?
A. The things that are beyond my control, the bureaucratic things. The

present economic challenges and its impact.

Q. Do you think the pay scale is fair?
A. Yes.

Q. Does your job bring you fulfillment or personal satisfaction?
A. Yes.

Q. How would you rate your job satisfaction low, med, high?
A. High.

Q. Did your educational background prepare you for your job?
A. Academically, Yes. Realistically, No. Getting a Ph.D. does not prepare you pedagogically at all. My educational background did not explain the expectations of higher education. It does not prepare you for the reality of getting promotion and tenure. If I were to interview now, I would ask different questions than I did ten years ago.

Q. What level of independence does your job require?
A. Academia has an incredibly high level of independence. At my university, I can go days in without seeing other professors in my department.

Q. What special skills do you feel are necessary to be effective in this position?
A. You must be a good communicator. You must have standards and stick to them. It's hard, but you must do it.

Q. Does your job encourage continuing education?
A. It encourages professional development.

Q. Do you feel that the salary that you receive for your job is commensurate with the work that you do?
A. That's a tough one. I think that I get well paid, but others get more. It's a good salary.

Q. Does your job require yearly certification?
A. No.

Q. Do you feel that the public respects your position?
A. Yes.

Q. Do you feel that your position is understood by the public?
A. No, a lot of people, the public does not understand what we do beyond the classroom: publishing, research, community services and why we teach nine hours.

Q. Do you feel that your job makes a difference?
A. Yes.

Q. Does your job achieve its intended purpose?
A. Yes.

Q. Do you feel that you have job security?
A. Yes.

Q. What is the salary range for your occupation?
A. I don't have any idea. I don't know. There are many people making more than me and many making less.

INTERVIEWEE NUMBER 2
Name Optional: Mohammed Abdukareem
Position: **Correctional Guard**
Number of Years: 1

Q. How many hours a week do you typically work?
A. 50 hours.

Q. How many years do you have to work before retirement?
A. I do not intend to keep the job. I will work five more years at the most with everything considered.

Q. Does your position allow you quality time with your family?
A. No.

Q. Does your current position allow for promotion?
A. Yes, it does in a way, but it takes a long time. Plus, things are based on your evaluation. You cannot have a disciplinary infraction.

Q. What about location? Did you have a choice of where you would work?

A. No, but I move around a lot going to TMC (Truman Medical Center) when inmates get sick or need to be transported to other places such as court or to another jurisdiction.

Q. What is the level of risk associated with your job?

A. A lot of risk is involved, but it depends on the officer. One has to be careful and cautious in his daily operations. You must respect the inmates if you do not, you may get stabbed. The inmates do not care, they will take your life. They have nothing to lose so you must respect them.

Q. What personality traits do you believe are important for this position?

A. No drug involvement, must be drug free. It entails professionalism. If you are a scary person you are not fit to be on the job because you must interact with the inmates.

Q. What does your daily routine consist of?

A. Among others, I do the log book. It consists of the time we report to duty, the population count to see the number of inmates that are on the floor, feeding time, quiet time starts at 4:00 they must turn the t.v. off; provide inmates mop buckets to clean up at 5:00. After quiet time, if it is a day of visitation. Inmates are brought out if they have a visitor. Inmates lose visitation if contraband is found. Other inmates are taken out for programs and recreation. Some go to the law library. There are professional visits by lawyers. At 10:00 p.m., they are racked for bed. Those inmates who have built up points for incentives can stay up to 1:00 p.m. on the weekends.

Q. What do you like best about your job?

A. You learn from the inmates. You try to study them. You give them respect, and they respect you. You cannot talk to them any kind of way. I learn a lot about behavioral problems. I learn a lot from the job. I know all of the inmates' names on my floor. There are 169 inmates, but sometimes the number vary.

Q. What do you like least about your job?

A. Racism, a lieutenant (white) who has a woman CO. He gives the less risky job assignments to the whites. He puts black in high risk areas. Yesterday, the lieutenant put a black female in a high risk position while stating that he knows that she will not like it. Despite seniority, he ignores it and places white persons with less rank over minority officers.

Q. Do you think the pay scale is fair?
A. No, because we are risking our lives for just $11 per hour.

Q. Does your job bring you fulfillment or personal satisfaction?
A. No.

Q. How would you rate your job satisfaction low, med, high?
A. High, I do the job to the best of my ability to get out alive. Law enforcement officers do less and get paid more.

Q. Did your educational background prepare you for your job?
A. Yes.

Q. What level of independence does your job require?
A. It requires at least three officers on the floor, but sometimes they let one person do the job. They often leave one person in an area of work that requires three people. The other day, they had someone new from the academy working. They have no experience, they just look at you. Sometimes people are even hired without training at the academy. They are called "shadow."

Q. What special skills do you feel are necessary to be effective in this position?
A. None, because all my skills are related to running the facility. I only need the policies and procedures.

Q. Does your job encourage continuing education?
A. No, not really. Sometimes if you're in school, they will assist you. They may pay tuition. On the other hand, no because you could be drafted. For example, if someone calls in sick, you must work no matter what. The draft lists are made by the shift administrator. It could be delegated to the lieutenant to do. School does not matter at this point. I was once told by the manager of detention after being drafted that if I wanted to go to school go, but if I wanted my job,

I must stay and work.

Q. Do you feel that the salary that you receive for your job is commensurate with the work that you do?

A. No.

Q. Does your job require yearly certification?

A. Yes, we must re-certify after one year, especially at the shooting range. We must qualify or face termination if you have difficulty qualifying with the weapon.

Q. Do you feel that the public respects your position?

A. Yes, because when I have my uniform on people think that I am a police officer. When I approach a store, people show me respect.

Q. Do you feel that your position is understood by the public?

A. Not really. However, some who have been in jail do. More often than not, people ask me what I do. Some view me as a security officer.

Q. Do you feel that your job makes a difference?

A. Yes, it does because the job requires us to counsel inmates. Some officers do not, but I do. For example, two of three brothers were living on my floor. One got released and shot his free brother and girl friend. The one confined cried all day long. I counseled him because I thought he could commit suicide. I pulled him out of his room during quite time. I let him out into the day space. I took him to a holding cell so that I could watch him. He requested to call his mom, and it calmed him down.

Q. Does your job achieve its intended purpose?

A. It does.

Q. Do you feel that you have job security?

A. No, because innocent people get fired because they have problems with the lieutenants and captains. For example, a guard was ordered by the lieutenant and captain to take a drug test after he reported them for speaking to him in a nonprofessional manner. The officer failed to appear for the drug test owing to his car being repossessed. He went to work the day he was supposed to report for drug testing and was fired.

Q. What is the salary range for your occupation?

A. While I don't know what the captain makes, it is possible that some correctional guards could make up to 50k. Correctional officers can make a lot of money because they are always calling for help because of a lack of staff.

INTERVIEWEE NUMBER 3
Name Optional: **Badge 1929**
Position: **Female Police Officer KCPD**
Number of Years **3.5**

Q. How many hours a week do you typically work?

A. Between 40 to 50.

Q. How many years do you have to work before retirement?

A. I have 21.5 years before retirement. I see retiring in law enforcement, but not as a field police officer.

Q. Does your position allow you quality time with your family?

A. My family does not live here. I live alone. Since I get four days off per week, it allows me a social life.

Q. Does your current position allow for promotion?

A. Not at the current time, I would need to have four years on the job before I can be promoted to sergeant.

Q. What about location? Did you have a choice of where you would work?

A. No.

Q. What is the level of risk associated with your job?

A. It depends on the neighborhood, or area that I'm working. The level of risk is higher in some places.

Q. What personality traits do you believe are important for this position?

A. You naturally have to be a suspicious, or somewhat nosy person.

You have to be suspicious of others. You have to be brave and courageous, and be able to work well under stressful situations. You must be able to make life and death decisions in a split second.

Q. What does your daily routine consist of?

A. Going to roll call which lasts for approximately 30 minutes and then I check out my equipment. I load my car with my equipment. I inspect my vehicle for any new damage. And I go in service. I call the dispatcher using a car radio and tell her that I am ready to take calls. I'm working. I drive around looking for crime and when a call comes in, I'm dispatched and I go to the call. I go to calls all night, or do other things like check out the drug dealers on the corners, or traffic violations, or any other suspicious activities I see.

Q. What do you like best about your job?

A. Helping people who want to be helped. Helping victims of crime and preventing future crime from happening to innocent people.

Q. What do you like least about your job?

A. Not being appreciated by the community. No matter what I do, I am still not going to prevent crime from happening. I may prevent it from happening at that time and location, but I am not going to prevent it in general.

Q. Do you think the pay scale is fair?

A. No. I think anybody who is a police officer does not do it for the pay anyway. But, I know that I possibly risk my life everyday and it deserves more than 37k a year.

Q. Does your job bring you fulfillment or personal satisfaction?

A. At times, and those times are the times when I feel that I actually helped changed something for the better.

Q. How would you rate your job satisfaction: low, med, high?

A. Medium.

Q. Did your educational background prepare you for your job?

A. For the most part, but not all of my classes. At the same time, no education would have prepared me to become a police officer. You learn more by actually being on the streets doing the job.

Q.   What level of independence does your job require?

A.   I can choose to ride alone or to have a partner. The first year, I had a partner. The second year and a half, I rode by myself. Right now, I have a partner again. When alone, I rely on me. I play somewhat of a different role when I am by myself. I play a nonthreatening role to someone who could harm me. For example, when approaching multiple suspects who could have warrants and are known to be violent, I pretend not to have any interest in taking them into custody. However, after calling for back-up and it arrives, I take on a more aggressive role by letting the suspects know who has a warrant, and I make an arrest. When I'm with a partner, I am naturally aggressive, but I always keep in mind that no arrest is worth my life. So, if I see things are going bad or my life or my partner's life is in danger, I will get the suspects later, or the next time I see them.

Q.   What special skills do you feel are necessary to be effective in this position?

A.   As a female, I rely on my communication skills versus a male police officer who may revert more to his physical skills, but a good cop has both. You have to be able to communicate. To work the streets, you have to be in good physical condition, but there is much more to be added here – common sense is a good thing to have on the streets.

Q.   Does your job encourage continuing education?

A.   No. Well. Wait. Yes. I take that back. They offer specialized training classes for us to attend throughout the year. I said no initially because they use to have college reimbursement programs, but they are going to take it away during this month.

Q.   Do you feel that the salary that you receive for your job is commensurate with the work that you do?

A.   No, because my life is worth more than 37k.

Q.   Does your job require yearly certification?

A.   Yes, So many hours a year, but I don't know off the top of my head. You must take so many hours of in service training.

Q. Do you feel that the public respects your position?

A. In general yes, but it seems in the neighborhoods that I patrol everyday, they dislike the police and they don't want us there. They are disrespectful.

Q. Do you feel that your position is understood by the public?

A. Yes, people think that we can do a lot of things we can't. They don't realize that we have to go by laws that prevent us from solving certain crimes right away.

Q. Do you feel that your job makes a difference?

A. It makes a difference in the small area I work, but I don't think it makes a difference in the larger scheme of things. There is still going to be crime, drug dealers – whether there are police or not – they still are going to be there.

Q. Does your job achieve its intended purpose?

A. Yes, society hires us to confront criminals because they don't want to do it.

Q. Do you feel that you have job security?

A. Yes.

Q. What is the salary range for your occupation?

A. From about $30,000 to $150,000 for the chief's position.

INTERVIEWEE NUMBER 4
Name Optional: Thomas Kartman
Position: **Male Police Officer KCPD**
Number of Years 10

Q. How many hours a week do you typically work?

A. 40 plus, sometimes a lot more.

Q. How many years do you have to work before retirement?

A. 15

Q. Does your position allow you quality time with your family?

A. Not enough, I work a p.m. shift so I am not home when my son comes home from school.

Q. Does your current position allow for promotion?

A. Yes. After being on for the required three years, I am able to be promoted after passing a written examination and an assessment evaluation.

Q. What about location? Did you have a choice of where you would work?

A. No.

Q. What is the level of risk associated with your job?

A. Medium to high, every call or car stop has the potential to be a lethal force encounter. You just never know what will happen.

Q. What personality traits do you believe are important for this position?

A. Fairness, open mindedness, integrity, honesty, and a very good sense of humor.

Q. What does your daily routine consist of?

A. Patrol, stop cars, answer calls for service.

Q. What do you like best about your job?

A. It is never dull, if it becomes slow, I can make something happen.

Q. What do you like least about your job?

A. Writing reports, it is time consuming and often seems like it is for nothing.

Q. Do you think the pay scale is fair?

A. Yes, compared to other law enforcement agencies in my area, we are compensated well.

Q. Does your job bring you fulfillment or personal satisfaction?

A. Both, I enjoy making neighborhoods safe from a criminal element.

Q. How would you rate your job satisfaction low, med, high?

A. High.

Q. Did your educational background prepare you for your job?

A. No, I had no intention of becoming a police officer, it was something I fell into almost by incident. Therefore, I never took any type of criminal justice classes until I became a police officer.

Q. What level of independence does your job require?

A. High, I pretty much mined my own business until I run into something that requires a supervisor's direction.

Q. What special skills do you feel are necessary to be effective in this position?

A. Visual perception, the ability to pick up little things that people don't normally notice.

Q. Does your job encourage continuing education?

A. Yes, I am currently enrolled in college obtaining a B.S. in criminal justice.

Q. Do you feel that the salary that you receive for your job is commensurate with the work that you do?

A. I believe it is.

Q. Does your job require yearly certification?

A. Yes, on firearms training and physical restraint.

Q. Do you feel that the public respects your position?

A. Yes and no: Normal law abiding people do respect the police whereas the criminal element does not.

Q. Do you feel that your position is understood by the public?

A. By some people, I think it is misunderstood.

Q. Do you feel that your job makes a difference?

A. None at all, the criminal youth quickly take the place of the criminal adults who find their way into the prison system.

Q. Does your job achieve its intended purpose?

A. As much as it can.

Q. Do you feel that you have job security?

A. Yes, as far as benefits are concerned, I feel there is some stability.

Q. What is the salary range for your occupation?

A. It varies, especially when overtime work is involved. An officer can make pretty good money.

INTERVIEWEE NUMBER 5
Name Optional: Melissa
Position: **Crime Scene Investigator**
Number of Years: 6

Q. How many hours a week do you typically work?

A. 40 plus, but there is a lot of overtime. It varies depending on the weather, weekend, payday, a full moon, and even season of the year. We are especially busy during holidays. We are also busy in the summer when children are out of school.

Q. How many years do you have to work before retirement?

A. Whenever my age and the number of years, I have worked on the job total the number 80.

Q. Does your position allow you quality time with your family?

A. Yes, but it varies because of my rotating schedule. It takes away time from the family because the job is 24/7, it plays into it. Everybody finds the shift that works best for them. The overtime can be paid time or in leave. We get more days off per year than many others.

Q. Does your current position allow for promotion?

A. Not right now, but it will change in the future.

Q. What about location? Did you have a choice of where you would work?

A. No.

Q. What is the level of risk associated with your job?

A. For the most part, the crimes are already committed before we arrive. Officers have things under control when we show up to collect evidence. They take control of people. When we would sometimes leave and return the police remain there to protect us. We do not have guns. Sometimes the crime scene is calm but people's family members may bring violence to the scene. We sometimes deal with blood and the possibility of being shot. Sometimes we even wear bullet proof vests for protection. This occurred on 9/11 and New Years Eve.

Q.   What personality traits do you believe are important for this position?

A.   Commonsense and to be able to think outside of the box. One must be detailed oriented. Must think in a logical manner. Be able to see the bigger picture. Must follow guidelines on the job – evidence is always different.

Q.   What does your daily routine consist of?

A.   It varies on different shifts. We process vehicles and process bodies. When we process bodies on the day shift, we go to the morgue to collect evidence on suicides, homicides and decomposed bodies. We scrape fingernails for DNA. When we process cars, we collect fingerprints, and take pictures and search for evidence in the car. During the course of any day, we take pictures and document evidence. The night shift goes to the hospital to collect evidence. Sometimes we collect rape kits from nurses.

Q.   What do you like best about your job?

A.   That it is interesting – we get out. It is not an office job. You go to so many different types of things. It never gets boring because you are always learning something new. It's a lot of fun working the scene to figure out what happened. You get to corroborate evidence with eyewitness testimony.

Q.   What do you like least about your job?

A.   A lot of paper work is generated in detail. Report writing is tedious and time consuming. It is unpleasant to work scenes involving children. Normally, you try to not get emotionally involved, but when dealing with children or innocent victims, it gets tough. But you cannot cry in the presence of others. It is difficult not feeling sorry for kids as opposed to some gang banger. You try not to let yourself get personally involved. You must see the victim as a piece of evidence and not a person.

Q. Do you think the pay scale is fair?

A. I think that we make fairly good money for what we do. But, I would like more money.

Q. Does your job bring you fulfillment or personal satisfaction?

A. Yes.

Q. How would you rate your job satisfaction: low, med, high?

A. High. Evidence convicts the bad guy. It also clears the innocent and that brings me satisfaction.

Q. Did your educational background prepare you for your job?

A. No.

Q. What level of independence does your job require?

A. Yes, sometimes we work with partners especially in a homicide when the crime scene is extensive.

Q. What special skills do you feel are necessary to be effective in this position?

A. Open mindedness and commonsense. It helps to have good writing skills. Good communication skills are needed when being in court and working with other officers. We also need these skills because we teach classes to outside agencies that send detectives for training. We are also qualified to teach and give presentations at public and private schools.

Q. Does your job encourage continuing education?

A. Yes.

Q. Do you feel that the salary that you receive for your job is commensurate with the work that you do?

A. Yes, but it should be more. It would be nice if they paid more to people with higher education. Must obtain several levels of certification, but no monetary reward or incentive is given.

Q. Does your job require yearly certification?

A. Yes, photography and techniques to collect evidence.

Q. Do you feel that the public respects your position?
A. Yes, but they may not understand. I believe that the show C.S.I. misleads the public. Strangers often ask me about the job.

Q. Do you feel that your position is understood by the public?
A. They may get the gist, but they do not understand that we only collect evidence and it is out of our hands. The public does not understand how valuable the little pieces of evidence are.

Q. Do you feel that your job makes a difference?
A. Yes.

Q. Does your job achieve its intended purpose?
A. Yes.

Q. Do you feel that you have job security?
A. Yes.

Q. What is the salary range for your occupation?
A. At the low end, it is $33,000 and at the top end, it is $53,000.

INTERVIEWEE NUMBER 6
Name Optional: Kyle Mead
Position: **Chief of Security of the KC Community Center Correctional Treatment Unit**
Number of Years: 3

Q. How many hours a week do you typically work?
A. 45

Q. How many years do you have to work before retirement?
A. I really do not know.

Q. Does your position allow you quality time with your family?
A. Yes.

Q. Does your current position allow for promotion?
A. Yes.

Q. What about location? Did you have a choice of where you would work?

A. We do have some options about where we can work.

Q. What is the level of risk associated with your job?

A. It's relatively high because we do accept dangerous offenders and people with mental health problems. The potential exists for violence to occur.

Q. What personality traits do you believe are important for this position?

A. Empathy is extremely important — an understanding of responsibility to community. The job is not punitive but based on reintegration and treatment. Some officers believe that the clients (felons) should be treated badly, but we teach them that the clients should be treated with respect so that they can be successful.

Q. What does your daily routine consist of?

A. Going over office reports from the day before. I examine critical incident and emergency procedures that were put in place – suicide threats – fire drills. I read those documents. There is a walk through of the building (inspection) everyday – nothing too glamorous. The rest of my time is spent scheduling of the staff making sure the coverage and training is there. I also screen for new employees.

Q. What do you like best about your job?

A. I enjoy it all the way around. I believe we are providing a vital service to the community. I feel proud when clients do well. It's a very interesting population to work with. Their success is big when it is small to someone else. To get a job, find an apartment. For example, sex offenders have a lot of restrictions placed on them. When they accomplish their goals, it's really great.

Q. What do you like least about your job?

A. It's not particularly well paid. It makes staff turn over very high. Maintain employment moral is a constant challenge. It's very tedious work day in and day out. It takes a negative occurrence to create excitement.

Q. Do you think the pay scale is fair?

A. I work in a nonprofit agency. I believe the company does the best that it can do. The salary is not commensurate with the work done. It provides rewards that are not necessarily monetary.

Q. Does your job bring you fulfillment or personal satisfaction?

A. Most definitely.

Q. How would you rate your job satisfaction: low, med, high?

A. High. They have been willing to allow me opportunity to advance through education.

Q. Did your educational background prepare you for your job?

A. To a very small degree. My experience allowed me the opportunity to get this job.

Q. What level of independence does your job require?

A. Not a lot of independence. I must work with program managers, executive directors, and probation and parole officers.

Q. What special skills do you feel are necessary to be effective in this position?

A. The position requires an immense amount of organization, a very keen eye towards documentation. Time management skills and a tolerance for many different people. There is a lot of cultural diversity.

Q. Does your job encourage continuing education?

A. Yes.

Q. Do you feel that   the salary that you receive for your job is commensurate with the work that you do?

A. No.

Q. Does your job require yearly certification?

A. Must do first aid training. C.P.R. plus, mandatory training in the area of verbal judo and conflict resolution.

Q. Do you feel that the public respects your position?

A. No, because there is not much knowledge that we even exist. But when we do get noticed, it's negative publicity.

Q. Do you feel that your position is understood by the public?
A. No.

Q. Do you feel that your job makes a difference?
A. Yes, because it is helping to create a safer community. We are not looking at behavior modification. We address housing, employment, and parole board speculated treatment. The opportunity for change is certainly there. The choice is left to the client.

Q. Does your job achieve its intended purpose?
A. The majority of the time.

Q. Do you feel that you have job security?
A. Yes.

Q. What is the salary range for your occupation?
A. At the low end of the scale, $15,000, but at the high end, $65,000.

INTERVIEWEE NUMBER 7
Name Optional: Shell
Position: **Probation Officer** (Houston, Texas)
Number of Years: **8**

Q. How many hours a week do you typically work?
A. 40

Q. How many years do you have to work before retirement?
A. Probably between 15 to 20. However, I do not believe I will retire, I want to teach.

Q. Does your position allow you quality time with your family?
A. Yes.

Q. Does your current position allow for promotion?
A. Yes, but very rare.

Q. What about location? Did you have a choice of where you would work?
A. No.

Q. What is the level of risk associated with your job?
A. Very high – because I work with domestic violence offenders.

Q. What personality traits do you believe are important for this position?
A. Must be a peoples person and have a peaceful disposition, but you must be firm sometime.

Q. What does your daily routine consist of?
A. Dealing with paperwork, casework, interviewing defendants, paperwork, answering telephones calls from defendants. Occasionally, you must conduct urine tests and do computer work.

Q. What do you like best about your job?
A. Imparting a difference in somebody's life.

Q. What do you like least about your job?
A. I wish it could be more safety oriented. Domestic violence offenders are trigger happy people. I wish it could be more safe for officers. There is no metal detectors so a person could bring a gun to my office. You never know if a person has a gun. The department is not geared toward safety.

Q. Do you think the pay scale is fair?
A. Heck, No.

Q. Does your job bring you fulfillment or personal satisfaction?
A. Yes.

Q. How would you rate your job satisfaction low, med, high?
A. Medium.

Q. Did your educational background prepare you for your job?
A. No.

Q. What level of independence does your job require?

A. You work alone, but you are part of a team. As far as your cases go, you supervise your own cases. I am the only person who works with my defendants.

Q. What special skills do you feel are necessary to be effective in this position?

A. You gotta have a limited amount of computer skills. You have to answer the phone in a professional manner. You got to have organizational skills. You have to be a peoples person. You gotta be willing to go the extra mile for the person. You can't be closed minded because these people have issues other than probation – their backgrounds, some have nowhere to stay.

Q. Does your job encourage continuing education?

A. No, but it is based on your supervisor. Sometimes supervisors can be flexible, but not the department. They never pay for it.

Q. Do you feel that the salary that you receive for your job is commensurate with the work that you do?

A. No.

Q. Does your job require yearly certification?

A. Yes. After the first year, you have to go through Community Supervision Officer Certification. After this, you just need 40 hours of training in the area of choice to help improve your job performance.

Q. Do you feel that the public respects your position?

A. Yes.

Q. Do you feel that your position is understood by the public?

A. No, because we get a lot of calls from people to make arrests and that's not the way it works.

Q. Do you feel that your job makes a difference?

A. Yes, because you get cards back, phone calls and some defendants tell you.

Q. Does your job achieve its intended purpose?

A. I do not know, because I do not have the statistics on the success rates.

Q. Do you feel that you have job security?

A. Yes, because criminals will keep committing crimes. I know that it's bad to say.

Q. What is the salary range for your occupation?

A. Officers start with 25K but the high end is in the 40s.

INTERVIEWEE NUMBER 8

Name Optional: Professor Anderson
Position: **Retired Federal Bureau of Investigation Agent**
Number of Years: **29**

Q. How many hours a week do you typically work?

A. What is unique with the FBI and maybe a lot of federal law enforcement agencies is that we have a base pay but than they have overtime pay that's almost guaranteed. I also don't know if you're familiar with that. Basically, the FBI agents get another 25% of their base salary once they get out in the field. Basically, that says we can call you anytime, any place, for any number of hours that we want to. The way to qualify to make sure that the government got their monies worth. The average agent works at least 50 hours.

Q. How many years do you have to work before retirement?

A. I retired in July of 1999.

Q. Does your position allow you quality time with your family?

A. Yes, it did, like in any law enforcement job. At least most of my friends and myself found out we got so enthused about the job, but after a while you realize you have to make time for your family, but investigation sometimes can get you going, but I learned after a while, it took me awhile to learn that family is more important.

Q. Does your current position allow for promotion?

A. Yes.

Q.   What about location? Did you have a choice of where you would work?

A.   The way it works in the FBI is that after you graduate from the FBI academy, your first assignment, you don't have a choice in. When I came in, they usually sent you to a small office for about two years. Then they sent you to a larger office. Then it is based on the seniority system, you get on an office of preference list. If you want to go to New York, we will help you in a hurry, if you want to go to Mobile, get in line. You know, when there is a vacancy. What's different now a day, is that many of the new agents are getting a lot closer to home and they're not transferred as much because it is just too expensive, the average cost of moving an agent and their family when I was in was $50,000 because now a day, we pay your real estate fees, home moving expenses, when I first came into the FBI, they didn't do that so their transfer policy has changed and agents don't get transferred as much as they used to now a days.

Q.   What is the level of risk associated with your job?

A.   Well, like any other job in law enforcement, if you're carrying a weapon and dealing with violent criminals, the potential is always there. There is also a potential there for getting hurt, getting shot, or getting killed. Nowhere near what a patrol officer or a highway patrol officer would be at risk of, but certainly the potential is there. I've had one friend killed in the line of duty. That has risen in the FBI over the years because of violent crime, but it's always there and you got to face it. That's the first thing that I tell people that want to go into law enforcement, have you thought about that.

Q.   What personality traits do you believe are important for this position?

A.   First, integrity, fidelity, loyalty to your country. A commitment to do the job right within the parameters of our legal system, and the biggest thing is you got to be able to talk to people. The big thing I would say is you got to be able to talk to people – you got to go out and, the whole job, well, an important part of the job is getting information. If you don't know how to treat people right, you don't know how to talk to people, you are going to be behind the eight ball. Some people it takes them some time to learn to do that. Myself, I was a shy person but after some time, you learn to get information.

Q. What does your daily routine consist of?

A. That was the good part about the FBI, you might have a day plan, you walk into the office and there might be a bank robbery or a kidnapping, or a 911, or some agent needs help on an interview that needs two agents. Basically, you work investigations on a priority basis, what who needs this US attorney needs this information. Next week, if he does, that's what I am going to do. If there's a bank robbery that's going to take precedence. So, any variety of things could happen. The beauty about the FBI is that they have about 270 violations we cover all the way from bank robberies to civil rights to police brutality, so every day was different.

Q. What do you like best about your job?

A. Variety, doing good for people, putting bad guys in jail. Helping people that had been victims of crime. Testifying in court, just being a good part of the criminal justice system.

Q. What do you like least about your job?

A. I guess from a personal standpoint, I saw in the FBI people could rise to more powerful positions by just going through the steps and being willing to be transferred around and spend time at FBI headquarters. And I blame myself and some of my friends for that because we didn't want to go through that with our families. The bureaucracy of the FBI at FBI head quarters was sometimes brought out at hearings and even recently.

Q. Do you think the pay scale is fair?

A. More than fair, I never thought being from a middle to lower class family, I never thought – I was making six figures when I retired. I would even say, the average street agent is probably making 80k, and the retirement is excellent.

Q. Does your job bring you fulfillment or personal satisfaction?

A. Absolutely, no doubt about it.

Q. How would you rate your job satisfaction – low, med, high?

A. Very high, it was the best job I ever had. The only reason that I retired was that federal law enforcement requires you to retire at age 57. Anyone who carries a gun in federal law enforcement has to retire at age 57. It use to be 55, there was some talk in Congress about moving it back to 60, but it's 57 now.

Q. Did your educational background prepare you for your job?

A. I would say to some extent. I went to school (college) played football. I was actually a business major, so that helped, but I think my personal background – growing up in an urban city like Detroit that helped me more than anything. I knew how to handle myself out there, I wasn't intimidated by people. I grew up in a diverse cultural and racial background. I say that that helped me more than anything helped.

Q. What level of independence does your job require?

A. A lot of independence, that's the nature of the job. If you were an FBI agent, you have 20 cases or 30 cases. You work those cases the way you decide to. You might work them differently than I would. The only person you really would answer to would be your immediate supervisor. A lot independence on the job.

Q. What special skills do you feel are necessary to be effective in this position?

A. Being able to talk to people, being proactive, being self-confident, having a presence of yourself not to be intimidated. Also, to be empathetic. Those are the skills I think are important. I think writing skills are important. I tell my students that probably 60% of the work is going to be after you get the information. You got to put it on paper, that report will go to the Assistant U.S. Attorney, it might end up on the defense attorney, the courts, so a good liberal arts education is important. Handle the job professionally.

Q. Does your job encourage continuing education?

A. What we did in the FBI, we had in service training, so we would have a variety of classes the agents would go back to the FBI academy for let's say interviewing. Let's say, he wanted to be a hostage negotiator. No formal education, but a lot of in service type training. I elected to go back and get my master's degree when I became a supervisor because I didn't think I was prepared, nor did the FBI prepare me to get into a management position. I would say that would be the shortcoming that I saw for the FBI is if you're a good agent, they assume you would be a good supervisor. Which quite frankly, a lot of business and law enforcement agencies do.

That's a big difference when you go on the other side of management.

Q. Do you feel that the salary that you receive for your job is commensurate with the work that you do?

A. I think I was more than rewarded. I liked the job so much that money wasn't a factor. The pay is very good, I thought so.

Q. Does your job require yearly certification?

A. We had a performance evaluation system where you got rated each year. From the stand point of physical and firearms, we had to qualify with a weapon at least four times a year. And physical, we had to take a physical examination – do some running and stuff like that. No testing, I think what they're doing now which I think we should have been doing is random or yearly polygraph tests because of these agents that have been convicted of espionage. They ask specific questions such as have you used drugs in the past years. Have you provided top secret information to a foreign intelligence agency.

Q. Do you feel that the public respects your position?

A. Yes, I think it went down a little, but I still think it is very high in law enforcement. The public for the most part, respects law enforcement – and particularly, the FBI.

Q. Do you feel that your position is understood by the public?

A. Not all the time. When I became a supervisor, I talked a lot in public and on radio talk shows, with the media. I'd go off to meetings of the American Legions and stuff like that. In fact, we're doing a presentation this spring on counterterrorism and the public perception, and I don't think the public knows what we have been doing in the intelligence field over the years so I am going to basically explain to them what I did from 1970 to 1999, and we are trying to get some spokespersons in the FBI to tell the group what's changed since 9/11 particularly in the intelligence field, I don't think the public knows what we can do, what we can't do.

Q. Do you feel that your job makes a difference?

A. Yes, I do. I took some killers off the streets, put some white collar people that wear suits and ties to work in jail that deserved to be there. I think that I even turned the life of a couple of people around that – a guy I put in jail for murder – he turned his life around.

Q. Does your job achieve its intended purpose?

A. I think so. I'd be surprised if any FBI or anyone in law enforcement would say his job was a waste of time. What you got to be careful about. I think it mainly happens with uniform police officers in large cities. Police officers start to view everyone as the enemy – us against them, but I didn't experience that in the FBI.

Q. Do you feel that you have job security?

A. Yes, absolutely in law enforcement.

Q. What is the salary range for your occupation?

A. I am going to guesstimate the average agent coming out of training school is going to be at 50 to 60k starting. I am guessing the high end of an experienced agent with 10 to 15 years will probably be making 80k to 85k range. They will get 50% of that at retirement. The supervisors and managers are making six figures. When I left, I was making 112k. That was real good money, and I didn't feel that I should be making that much, but it was the system or the structure that I was in.

INTERVIEWEE NUMBER 9
Name Optional: **TPR D.W. Schubert**
Position: **State Trooper/ Highway Patrol**
Number of Years: **4**

Q. How many hours a week do you typically work?

A. It varies, but it's probably 40. We always get comp time.

Q. How many years do you have to work before retirement?

A. I will be eligible in 20 years.

Q. Does your position allow you quality time with your family?

A. Yes, it can be tough at times because there are like with any job times when you miss things because of work. There are Saturdays when I am at some event and not at home doing things with my family. For the most part, it is not that bad. We work two days and have nights off.

Q. Does your current position allow for promotion?

A. You are automatically promoted to trooper first-class after three years. After five years, you're promotable from first class to corporal. A year in grade, you're eligible for sergeant. Because a lot of folk are retiring, others are being promoted.

Q. What about location? Did you have a choice of where you would work?

A. You put in three choices or reasons. I was given an opportunity to say why I wanted the first choice and it was so that I could finish a college degree. They always accommodate you, but they have a mission.

Q. What is the level of risk associated with your job?

A. I don't think you think about it. It's pretty high. It's there when you go to work everyday. You just don't know if you're gonna come back in, and it may never happen in your career, the possibility is there.

Q. What personality traits do you believe are important for this position?

A. The first thing is integrity, treating people the way you want to be treated and having common sense.

Q. What does your daily routine consist of?

A. What ever comes up. We have three different shifts, 24 hours a day. I go in and check email, return a multitude of phone calls. Day shifts at 6, 7, 8, and 9. Someone is always on at 6:00. There is a lot of paper work. We will react to what's present. Typically, you get caught up on accidents and if you have time, you go and negotiate action. One thing that differs us from the police is that we have a lot of proactive time.

Q. What do you like best about your job?

A. Freedom, your car is in your drive way. You go to work. You get in your car, turn the radio on and call in. You can go out there at one minute and write speeding tickets, and decide the next thing -- you want to be a drug investigator, go ahead and knock yourself out. You want to look for drunks, go right ahead. You can wander wherever you want within your zone. You're not in an office. You're out there getting fresh air.

Q.   What do you like least about your job?

A.   Having to give a death notice or a criminal investigation dealing with a death, especially giving notice to a family – it's rough.

Q.   Do you think the pay scale is fair?

A.   No, in our line of work, I don't think that it's ever fair. That's just the same for teacher.

Q.   Does your job bring you fulfillment or personal satisfaction?

A.   Yes, I say based on all the jobs I've ever had since I was 18, this is about the most difficult. I love this, I wouldn't want to do anything else.

Q.   How would you rate your job satisfaction: low, med, high?

A.   Medium to high. There are things that can be modified. Some things can be improved. Sometimes you get caught up in things, but if you step back and look at things, it's a good job.

Q.   Did your educational background prepare you for your job?

A.   Personally, I want to say yes and no. I think there's a big division between theoretical and practical. What I learned in the classroom and even at the academy was great and theoretical, but getting out here is a whole different world. Only experience can prepare you for some of the things you come across. For example, when you're out there, you have to make decisions real quick and requires more of what you learn on the job. In class, you can debate, out there, you have to make that decision in a fraction of a second. You have to make the right decision or it could be something detrimental to the agency or yourself. It's a little different.

Q.   What level of independence does your job require?

A.   Total. For some, it may depend on your people assisting you. The radio operator, for the most part, when it comes down to it, you're the one taking care of you. Your backup is 20 minutes away. You're there by yourself. You have to be independent. You're by yourself. In some cases, you need to be in a metropolitan area when you call for backup, 40 cars show up in a matter of seconds. That kind of depends, but there's a lot of help, but when you're alone, it places a lot of responsibility on you.

Q. What special skills do you feel are necessary to be effective in this position?

A. Time management, and be able to believe in yourself. Be able to prioritize things. You're out there working and you may come across something, now you got a report to do, but you're the only police out there and they're stopping cars. You want to get out there, but you got to get this report done by a certain time because it got to get to a prosecutor office and have a warrant filed on it or something. So, I think time management comes in, you have to lay out those priorities. Interpersonal skills — a lot of things, it's the way you present yourself or the way you present a question, or a conversation has a lot to do with the result of the conversation. When you talk to somebody to calm down or do what you need them to do effectively versus if you don't know how to talk to somebody they may become aggressive. The days of being a police officer walking a beat and getting up there and doing what ever are over. We are asked to do a multitude of things besides enforce the laws, people expect us to be a medic, lawyer, counselor, anything. You have to learn to put that together. The job is always changing. For example, reports and the laws.

Q. Does your job encourage continuing education?

A. Yes, tuition reimbursement are set aside for undergraduates, the agency pays 100% for the grade of an A. It pays 75% for a B. It pays 50% for a C, and pays nothing for a grade below a C. For graduate work, it pays 100% for an A. It pays 50% for a B and nothing for a grade that's below that. Promotion is not linked to education, but upper management is. My captain and lieutenants have masters degrees. I am looking to get my masters.

Q. Do you feel that the salary that you receive for your job is commensurate with the work that you do?

A. Is there a dollar amount that you can put on what we do, probably not, but is there a dollar amount you can put on the happiness of the satisfaction from helping people. Nobody come into this for the salary.

Q. Does your job require yearly certification?

A. Yes, firearms, three times a year. We also do first aid, critical responses, cultural diversity, terrorism, and domestic violence. There's something every year.

Q. Do you feel that the public respects your position?

A. Yes, I say that having come from a previous agency to this one, I can't tell you the number of times, I've stopped a car and people have said thank you, not for just giving a ticket or taking someone to jail. They're saying thank you for not disrespecting or degrading me. I guess they thank me for being professional. I think they respect us depending on the area you work or the region you work in. It can reflect the amount of respect they actually show. There is no doubt the respect is there, but some people show it more. They will go out of the way to get your attention to say hi to you. The more metro area you get, the less they know about you. Rural areas are aware of you.

Q. Do you feel that your position is understood by the public?

A. No, I don't think so. People ask questions about my job. For example, my neighbors said that she didn't know that I could stop cars in the city. A lot of people don't know that we have investigative wings that we have search teams, aviation divisions, folks don't know any of that stuff. The every day citizen don't know what we do. We go beyond giving speeding tickets.

Q. Do you feel that your job makes a difference?

A. I say yes in that if I can have my car on that highway, it might prevent an accident. I feel like I have done something positive. I have arrested intoxicated people before and talked to them about their alcohol use told them what it's doing to them. I can think of two people who brought it to my attention that they have given up alcohol. We educate the public on the dangers of drinking. It changes some people's behavior. I have gone to schools and given presentations after it was over, I had a teacher to call me and said I have a young student who never thought about a career of being a police officer until now. They realize that we are everyday people.

Q. Does your job achieve its intended purpose?

A. I think it does, on a smaller scale. It makes people think about what they do before getting into their vehicle.

Q. Do you feel that you have job security?
A. Yes, with the economy being what it is. There is always going to be something going on. Unfortunately, someone will always be doing something wrong. That will secure we will have a job.   The retirement is very good.

Q. What is the salary range for your occupation?
A. The low end for a trooper, a recruit in the academy makes about $30,996. The high end is what the colonel makes which is about 86 to 89k. There is only one person who gets that. But, with each promotion a salary can increase. Salary is based on the number of years and not necessarily one's rank.

INTERVIEWEE NUMBER 10
Name Optional: **Jenni**
Position: **Chief Duty Juvenile Officer**
Number of Years: **5**

Q. How many hours a week do you typically work?
A. Between 50 to 60.

Q. How many years do you have to work before retirement?
A. I can actually retire at 80 now. The state system counts age plus the years of service.

Q. Does your position allow you quality time with your family?
A. Yes.

Q. Does your current position allow for promotion?
A. Yes.

Q. What about location? Did you have a choice of where you would work?
A. Yes.

Q. What is the level of risk associated with your job?
A. Very minor for this particular position. I have very little contact with

clients. At the present time, I am primarily a supervisor.

Q. What personality traits do you believe are important for this position?

A. I think you have to be ethical, and have a good work ethic. Its imperative that you be willing to do what it takes to get the job done. So, honesty is always a good characteristic. I think its like most jobs any of the technical aspects you can learn, but if you're not an ethical or responsible person, you shouldn't be applying for these kinds of jobs.

Q. What does your daily routine consist of?

A. Usually when I get here, I check detention I go back to make sure we have a complete night in detention. From there, I review the referrals or the things that have come in overnight like intakes. Look at and sign those reports. Many days we have court to over see all of that. Meet with staff as needed to review cases. I pay all bills. I do all the administrative things like make sure we have all the necessary things ordered. I basically do all of the computer stuff here. Management, the network — I wrote the database, I take care of all that, so that's my day.

Q. What do you like best about your job?

A. I like the fact that I think I can still have a positive effect on kids and where we're going with things. I think the absolute best thing is that the buck stops with me. Things are going to be based on how well I do my job. I like being in that position and holding myself to a high level of accountability.

Q. What do you like least about your job?

A. The politics are always difficult. I think that lack of resources is always frustrating. Dealing with personnel issues is always frustrating as well. When I came into this, I knew a heck a lot about managing cases, and I was able to do a fairly decent job of that, but it did not prepare me to be boss and manage the personnel issues and personalities and all the little things that go on have nothing to do with case management that you're responsible for.

Q. Do you think the pay scale is fair?

A. Yes, I do.

Q.   Does your job bring you fulfillment or personal satisfaction?
A.   Yes, I think so.

Q.   How would you rate your job satisfaction: low, med, high?
A.   I would say high.

Q.   Did your educational background prepare you for your job?
A.   No.

Q.   What level of independence does your job require?
A.   A tremendous amount of independence. You have to be able to make decisions from both an analytical perspective as well as decisive at times.

Q.   What special skills do you feel are necessary to be effective in this position?
A.   I think you have to have common sense. I am not sure that's a special skill, but not every body I deal with possesses that trait. And I think you have to have a reasonableness about you. I think you have to be able to deal with people of every shape, size, and origin. You have to be able to communicate clearly with everyone from a judge to a seven year old kid you see here.

Q.   Does your job encourage continuing education?
A.   Yes.

Q.   Do you feel that the salary that you receive for your job is commensurate with the work that you do?
A.   Yes, I do.

Q.   Does your job require yearly certification?
A.   No, the only requirement that we have is a standard 40 hour of on going training per year.

Q.   Do you feel that the public respects your position?
A.   I think so.

Q.   Do you feel that your position is understood by the public?
A.   No, I think they are a little afraid of what I do, but they don't understand.

Q. Do you feel that your job makes a difference?
A. Yes.

Q. Does your job achieve its intended purpose?
A. Yes.

Q. Do you feel that you have job security?
A. Yes.

Q. What is the salary range for your occupation?
A. $27, 000 starting to about $54, 000.

INTERVIEWEE NUMBER 11
Name Optional: **Lora Burk**
Position: **District Administrator of Probation and Parole(District 5)**
Number of Years: **2.5 years**

Q. How many hours a week do you typically work?
A. It's about 40 hours a week job, but there are weeks, my position you get quote "comp" time. You just do whatever you need to do to complete the task, so if I need to work 50 hours, I need to work 50 hours. So, I am paid a salary and don't get compensated for over time. My position doesn't the other positions do in, most agencies.

Q. How many years do you have to work before retirement?
A. We're 80 and out, so my years of service plus my age need to equal 80 for full retirement.

Q. Does your position allow you quality time with your family?
A. Absolutely, it has to, most definitely. With our sick leave policy, if my children are sick, I can take sick leave instead with a lot of companies, you have to be sick yourself before you can take sick leave or we have flex time because our job is not a Monday through Friday, 8 to 5 job and for the most part while I don't get comp time, I can be flexible I can come in at noon and work until 8 and then I can go and read to my kids class for a couple of hour, if I want to. It's a definite benefit.

Q. Does your current position allow for promotion?

A. Yes, from District Administrator, it will be Regional Administrator and I would have like right now. I am in charge of a whole district. I have about 27 employees, and the next step up would be a region with several different districts which that their district administrators would report to. Right now, my boss has 7 of us that report to him.

Q. What about location? Did you have a choice of where you would work?

A. Yes and no, these positions become available not very frequently because usually you can't hold for a long time. There are not a lot of places you can go on this level and the chances for promotion if you want to stay on the probation/parole side are not many places above that, but when there is one open, I would have to put in at that district. If I got it, I would have to relocate or transfer. Just so happens, I have done most of my career in this district.

Q. What is the level of risk associated with your job?

A. With the District Administrators job, I guess my risk is a lot lower than probably the probation officer because I don't have as much direct exposure with the offenders. However, I did just get back from the fields going out with my officer and seeing how he conducts his home visits and how he interacts with the offenders. So, experience wise, I guess it is still there. But I have never felt very threaten in any of the positions that I've had with the agency.

Q. What personality traits do you believe are important for this position?

A. A lot of the things, it takes to be a probation officer. You have to be pretty strong willed, not easily influenced from outside influences from offenders. You need to be fair, honest, understanding, and compassionate. You need to be able to look at a situation and impose your views or beliefs. That's really important probably more so with officers as well as a supervisor.

Q. What does your daily routine consist of?

A. I do administrative duties. I am in charge of personnel, lots of report writing. I am responding to requests from higher ups. What is my budget, how much money have I spent, what's the status of my pool of cars. I manage a fleet of cars. Employee background checks, I do a lot of responding to email. I do a lot of reporting writing — summarizing duties and activities or things that we have done in our district. Putting out fires, working with officers when they have an emergency when their direct supervisor may not be available so they come to me and we have to handle warrant situations or what do we do with offenders that did authorization for more than what they can authorize as an officer.

Q. What do you like best about your job?

A. Is that it's different everyday. With all the positions that I have had with the agency, from Clerical I up, but it's never the same. I don't know when I come in from one day to the next, while the core job duties are the same, each different experience that I have or each different offender just when you think you're seen it all – I never experienced that before. And that's really the same way in management. Coupled with that is the challenge and exciting that it's never boring is the flexibility – it allows me to be mom and while I can do that, I am very much a type of career person. But my family is very important and state employment allows me flexibility and I am grateful.

Q. What do you like least about your job?

A. I don't believe that the District Administrator has as much control over personnel issues as I would like to see them have. We do not have as much hiring and firing authority. It's all pretty much a merit system and we're bound. It takes a lot to terminate an employee or on the same hand, it takes a lot to get special acknowledgment for workers or we can't give them a bonus for doing an outstanding job for going above and beyond the call of duty. So from an administrative point of view, that's the thing that I like the least is that we don't have hardly any control of those situations.

Q. Do you think the pay scale is fair?

A. I think that we need to make more money and the District Administrator all of us need more money on the Missouri side, I think we are underpaid, I haven't looked for another job either.

Q. Does your job bring you fulfillment or personal satisfaction?

A. Absolutely.

Q. How would you rate your job satisfaction: low, med, high?

A. High.

Q. Did your educational background prepare you for your job?

A. My job right now, No. Probably not, it prepared me for the steps I needed to get to this point. It did not prepare me for the management side.

Q. What level of independence does your job require?

A. A lot, you have to be pretty independent to do this. You have to be thick skinned because we have to make decisions daily that people don't like. It took me a long time to get acclimated to that the first year, making decisions that staff may or may not like. So, we have to be independent thinkers to do that. Pull yourself again and say that I'm doing this for the best for this district, and not for the special interest of one, two, or three people.

Q. What special skills do you feel are necessary to be effective in this position?

A. Organized, you need to be highly organized to manage and facilitate a budget in the district to take care of the pool of cars. I need to be able to realize the actions that I do today what long term effect they are going to have and I am taking the district in the right direction. Am I meeting the goals of the agency while considering the needs of all my staff members as well?

Q. Does your job encourage continuing education?

A. Yes, we do. We use to give educational leave — but no longer do that, but you can work flextime. We allow flex scheduling. Several staff members take advantage of that. We have educational reimbursement. Diverse funds but even in today's budget cuts ever since 9/11, we have not lost the educational funding to this point. We do encourage higher education.

Q. Do you feel that the salary that you receive for your job is commensurate with the work that you do?

A. No.

Q. Does your job require yearly certification?

A. Not the actual job, but to secure a firearm. Yes, we have that's an aspect of the job, but its not mandated. Safety certification, yes, we have to do that and we all have to pass that certification. But, there is no professional licensing certification, but if we cannot pass the safety component, the physical, verbal judo and safety skills quarterly, we cannot continue.

Q. Do you feel that the public respects your position?

A. I think that's different in every area you go. In this district, I believe that that is the case. I have some really good staff that have worked really hard with their local law enforcement, and I know we are well respected in that area, but they know what we do and we network with them. For example, the courts, DFS, juvenile office and those kinds of things. I think we are respected. I think sometimes general average every day citizens do not have any idea what we do and while we do a pretty good job of advertizing that or if our offenders are doing some special program, we try to get some publicity for it. I still think we're probably a mystery to some people. But still that is not the case in every district.

Q. Do you feel that your position is understood by the public?

A. It depends on how you define public. No, probably not for the most part. Now the people who work closely with us or know someone that works there. But when I go to church, some one may ask, well what do you do? Most of the time, they think we're juvenile officers. That's really a poor subject for most of us, especially for a woman and we say we work at probation and patrol. We have these kids, they almost always think we're juvenile officers. We are like, no we're not, we are adult probation and parole officers.

Q. Do you feel that your job makes a difference?

A. Yes, I do. I don't think it makes a difference as often as I would like it. But every once in a while, you see an offender that comes back or keep in touch or touch base with us. You get a letter out of the blue from someone that says, you made a difference to me or you were really tough, but this is what I learned and thank you for doing that, but I wish those were not as few and far between. I wish they were a little closer together.

Q. Does your job achieve its intended purpose?

A. Yes.

Q. Do you feel that you have job security?

A. Absolutely, while I feel we are salary wise not compensated the way we should, I do believe we have a sense of job security that you don't have in corporate America. So, to me you have to look at the whole picture, I have flexibility. I have job security. I don't make as much money, but I am going to have a job tomorrow.

Q. What is the salary range for your occupation?

A. We all are going to make about the same. It's a merit system here, so, it's not like anybody is going to get a raise unless you have "Joe Blow" who have been with us for 20 years and they were part of the merit raise earlier, but we earn around 40k.

ABBREVIATIONS

ABD	All But Dissertation
ABF	American Bar Foundation
ACJS	Academy of Criminal Justice Sciences
AOC	Administrative Office of the Courts
APT	Adolescent Portable Therapy
ASC	American Society of Criminology
ATF	Bureau of Alcohol, Tobacco, and Firearms
ATV	All Terrain Vehicle
BCIS	Bureau of Citizenship and Immigration Services
BLM	Bureau of Land Management
CALEA	Commission on Accreditation for Law Enforcement Agencies
CHET	Customs High Endurance Tracker
CIA	Central Intelligence Agency
CO	Correctional Officer
CPR	Cardiopulmonary Resuscitation
DEA	Drug Enforcement Administration
DNA	Deoxyribonucleuic Acid
FLETC	Federal Law Enforcement Training Center
DOJ	Department of Justice
DOT	Department of Transportation
EEO	Equal Employment Opportunity
FAA	Federal Aviation Administration
FAM	Federal Air Marshall
FAMTP	Federal Air Marshall Training Program
FBI	Federal Bureau of Investigation
FinCEN	Financial Crimes Enforcement Network
GED	General Education Diploma
HCRC	Habeas Corpus Resource Center
HUD	Housing and Urban Development
IAP	Intensive Aftercare Program
INS	Immigration and Naturalization Services
INTERPOL	International Police
INS	Immigration and Naturalization Services
JD	Juris Doctorate
NCIC	National Crime Information Center
NCJJ	National Center for Juvenile Justice
NCOVR	National Consortium of Violence Research

NCVS	National Crime Victimization Survey
NIJ	National Institute of Justice
OOI	Office of Intelligence
PERF	Police Executive Research Forum
Ph.D.	Doctor of Philosophy
PINS	Persons in Need of Supervision
POST	Peace Officers Standards and Training
ROR	Release on Recognizance
TSA	Transportation Security Administration
SPS	Security Protective Service
SRS	Self-Report Surveys
UCR	Uniform Crime Reports
USCS	United States Customs Service
VWAP	Victim-Witness Assistance Program

INDEX

ABOUT THE AUTHORS

James F. Anderson is Associate Professor of Criminal Justice and Criminology at the University of Missouri at Kansas City in the Department of Sociology, Criminal Justice and Criminology. He received his doctorate in Criminal Justice from Sam Houston State University and a master's degree in Criminology from Alabama State University. He has published numerous articles and four books: Boot Camps: An Intermediate Sanction; Legal Rights of Prisoners: Cases and Comments; Criminal Justice and Criminology: Concepts and Terms; and Criminological Theories: Understanding Crime in America.

Nancie J. Mangels is a doctoral fellow at the University of Missouri at Kansas City in the Department of Sociology, Criminal Justice and Criminology. She has co-authored one book, Criminal Justice and Criminology: Concepts and Terms and several articles in The Justice Professional and the Journal of Gang Research in the areas of evaluative bio-criminological research and hate groups and gangs. Her research interests include race and incarceration, gangs and hate groups, bio-crime studies, and criminal justice-related issues.

Laronistine Dyson is President, Chief Executive Officer and Executive Director of Residential Alternatives Inc. of Kentucky. She completed the Master of Arts degree in Interpersonal and Public Communication at Bowling Green State University. She has published four books: Boot Camps: An Intermediate Sanction; Legal Rights of Prisoners: Cases and Comments; Criminal Justice and Criminology: Concepts and Terms; and Criminological Theories: Understanding Crime in America. She also has to her credit over twenty-five articles in the areas of criminal justice, criminology, and psychology.